# SERIOUSLY FUNNY

## Graham Eastaugh

authorHOUSE®

*AuthorHouse™ UK Ltd.*
*500 Avebury Boulevard*
*Central Milton Keynes, MK9 2BE*
*www.authorhouse.co.uk*
*Phone: 08001974150*

F
Eastaugh,
Graham

*First published by AuthorHouse    11/18/2010*

*ISBN: 978-1-4520-5354-7 (sc)*

*This book is printed on acid-free paper.*

This book is dedicated to all friends and family who have supported me throughout many difficult years. It wouldn't have been possible without you. Many thanks. Also, thanks to all the girls who worked on Ward B28, Broomfield Hospital from June 2008 to January 2009. You were sensational.

# The Author

Graham Eastaugh was diagnosed with multiple sclerosis in 1983 at the age of twenty-two. As his condition deteriorated he became dependent on a wheelchair in 1989, and in 1996 had to take early retirement from his job with a local publishing company in Colchester, Essex. It was a couple of years after this when he began to write poetry which culminated in the publication of this book.

# Contents

# PC twaddle

Political correctness: it's driving me mad,
Some say it's good news, but I say it's bad,
What's the world coming to? All is absurd,
We can't speak our minds, and watch every word,
But I've had enough of this toeing the line,
I'm sick of ensuring my speech is benign,
But never again, 'cause I'm bucking the trend,
I'm bringing all talk of PC to an end,
I've always referred to a spade as a spade,
And never been scared of the comments I've made,
The Irish are Paddies, Italians are wops,
And Pakis are people who own corner shops,
A Scotsman's a Jock, and a German's a Kraut,
And a bird looks her best with her tits hanging out,
A homo's a poofter, a slapper's a bike,
A Scouser's a thief, and a lezzer's a dyke,
And what about people who say they're big-boned?
They're fat, for fuck's sake, but the truth is bemoaned,
Vertically challenged? Or just a short-arse?
Why talk in riddles? The whole thing's a farce,
So, as from today, I'll be speaking my mind,
I'm leaving my mealy-mouthed days all behind,
I've played the game once, and I'm not going back,
So, me become PC? I'd rather be black.

Graham Eastaugh 9/11/98

# Tales of the riverbank

Fish have no feelings; or so it's been claimed,
They never feel pain when horrifically maimed,
Fillet or batter them, do as you wish,
Try all you can, but you can't hurt a fish,
I've always been baffled by views such as these,
I wonder if anyone out there agrees?
But proof of this theory seems terribly frail,
It seems to me merely a fisherman's tale,
It's all very well to say fish feel no pain,
But how many fish have been asked in the main?
Have scientists over the years gathered quotes,
From fish saying hooks only tickle their throats?
It seems to me purely an easy way out,
Of keeping objections from coming about,
Suggestions of cruelty would soon lose their sting,
If someone has 'proven' they can't feel a thing,
But make your own mind up - they've feelings or not?
A fish simply can't be hurt, no matter what?
But here's a short story to help you decide,
I once called a woman a trout, and she cried.

Graham Eastaugh 24/1/00

# Gone with the wind

It tickled me pink when I let off a stink,
It came from my arsehole, you know,
It seemed really easy; a chicken jalfrezi,
Then, wallop! A fart I let go,
No ifs or buts, I was dropping my guts,
I'm always displaying my charms,
I'm ever so proud 'cause the fart was so loud,
It set off a couple of burglar alarms,
You can't say I sinned; I simply broke wind,
My stomach was feeling so rough,
Don't heap the blame on an innocent name,
'Cause even the Queen has to guff,
I hasten to mention the fart released tension,
So don't criticise me, I beg,
Though out on the street, my fart was discreet,
And most of the ripples I shook down my leg,
It happened so quick, I made myself sick,
Those curries can certainly reek,
As if I was cursed, to make matters worse,
I'd not had a shit for a week,
Don't think I'm coarse, for I'm full of remorse,
I wish that this tale wasn't true,
'Cause after the fart, just a second apart,
A 'tortoise' appeared and I then followed through.

Graham Eastaugh 4/2/99

3

# Sunny delight

The weather in Britain is fickle of kind,
And sometimes it plays funny tricks on the mind,
By making us see things that aren't really there,
I offer the following story to share:
I ventured outdoors but a few days ago,
To see unfamiliar people on show,
They didn't hold something unpleasant in store,
The truth is I'd probably seen them before,
The day was quite hot, and the sky really blue,
The change from the days before almost untrue,
Until then the spring had been rainy and cold,
But now was a different tale to be told,
The clothing that everyone wore had all changed,
Their outdoor apparel had been rearranged,
Gone were the raincoats and ankle-length skirts,
The temperature called for bare legs and T-shirts,
Each female on view looked a cracker at worst,
The front of my boxer shorts felt fit to burst,
The visions I saw drove me out of my wits,
Wherever I turned there was fanny and tits,
There seemed to be nothing but nipples about,
And one girl, I swear, nearly took my eye out,
It wasn't important what faces they'd got,
As long as their bits were on show, they were hot,
The miserable bag down the street looked superb,
And even the trouts made me drive off the kerb,
I had to keep blinking; I thought I was dreaming,
And even the twelve-year-old schoolgirls were steaming,
I felt quite confused but I couldn't mistake,
The difference a change in the weather can make,
The moment the sun shows its face for a bit...
And, bugger me, even a nun's looking fit!

Our eyesight betrays us should sunshine appear,
It happens sometimes more than ten times a year,
When even the plain janes look absolute crackers,
Disturbing the peace of inquisitive knackers,
So back to the point where my tale had begun,
Attraction is largely to do with the sun,
It's all about sunshine and getting enough,
I guess that's why Eskimo gals look so rough.

Graham Eastaugh 29/4/02

# War

Last night I awoke from a terrible dream,
I'd travelled through time back to 1916,
My mind took me back through the years whereupon,
I stood in a field on the banks of the Somme,
Knee-deep in water, I stood in a trench,
The atmosphere filled with a horrible stench,
The gunfire was deafening; terror was rife,
With death all around me, I prayed for my life,
How had I sunk to this awful abyss?
For nobody told me that war was like this,
I signed for the glory, but now felt beguiled,
My body was shaking; 1 cried like a child,
But then I came round; it was all in the mind,
My consciousness left all these nightmares behind,
But very soon after, I went back to sleep,
My dream took a quick chronological leap,
The dateline had moved ahead twenty-nine years,
An atom bomb realised all of my fears,
No one was spared, every child, woman, man,
A city destroyed in the heart of Japan,
Thousands of people were stripped of their flesh,
If only the human race started afresh,
We'd think of a way of avoiding this pain,
We'd never indulge in such horror again,
But sadly we would, and madly we will,
Till one day there's no one to pick up the bill,
We'll never have peace, for which most of us yearn,
We've had lots of lessons, but never quite learn,
My thoughts were just visions; for some they were real,
It's hard to imagine how war can appeal,
The passion for conflict's a mystery to me,
I hope I'm long gone when they start World War Three.

Graham Eastaugh 20/4/99

# A bolt from the blue

I was sitting at home, with little to do,
The weather was cold, so I didn't go out,
I thought about life, and was thinking things through,
How slight alterations of mind come about,
Now, I'm not as young as I once was, for sure,
However, it's so that I'm not really *old*,
But what happened next shook me right to the core,
I came to conclusions that turned my flesh cold,
I'd always believed I was young in the mind,
I'd not crossed the line where my youthfulness stops,
I moved with the times, and was never behind,
But everything changed watching Top of the Pops,
I thought to myself as I looked at the screen,
How everything sounds so incredibly loud,
And most of the artists look twelve or thirteen,
And look at the state of the twats in the crowd!
You can't hear the words, and they can't even sing,
And no one writes tunes you can hum any more,
You can't tell a he from a she, from a 'thing',
And aren't all these rap songs a terrible bore?
It suddenly hit me; I found out the truth,
And all my delusions were blown wide apart,
A half an hour's telly provided the proof,
And that was the day I became an old fart.

Graham Eastaugh 14/9/99

7

# Crime and punishment

I've always been someone to live and let live,
A good human being who's quick to forgive,
I try all I can to be honest and kind,
And live with a wholly unprejudiced mind,
But recent events turned my world upside down,
As now I appear crematorium-bound,
We all make mistakes in our lives now and then,
But *I* dropped a clanger I *won't* drop again,
I'd drawn a cartoon of a scene in a field,
Where Allah stood tall with his tackle revealed,
The Prophet Mohammed, to Allah's great shock,
Was down on his hands and knees, sucking his cock,
The rear of Mohammed was too cute to pass,
With Jesus Christ giving him one up the arse,
A senior rabbi was dressed as a tranny,
While eating a portion of roasted pig's fanny,
It suddenly dawned on me what I'd just done,
Depicting religion as figures of fun,
I'd probably upset both Christians and Jews,
Though figured my actions they'd likely excuse,
However, I'd got in a heck of a jam,
By deeply insulting the faith of Islam,
They'd issue a fatwah demanding my head,
They wouldn't relax till they'd witnessed me dead,
My body was trembling; I started to cry,
I'm not even fifty; I don't want to die,
I saw my demise as a terrible waste,
And all for a cartoon I'd scribbled in haste,
I thought of my loved ones, then drew a deep breath,
Preparing myself for my imminent death,
When out of the blue I awoke with a scream,
Thank Buddha! The whole tale was merely a dream.

Graham Eastaugh 19/6/07

# Bits and bobs and tits and knobs

The wonderful thing about fannies,
Is fannies are wonderful things,
There's not a lot to 'em, but blokes love to view 'em,
And feel all the pleasure they bring,
I can't say the same about willies,
They're not quite a sight for sore eyes,
They're ever so wrinkly, and horribly crinkly,
And many are lacking in size,
The opposite's true about knockers,
Just looking at them is a treat,
Their skin is quite smooth, and they're able to soothe,
And the nipples just make 'em complete,
That's never the case about knackers,
They're just there to cause men distress,
The more we get agile, the more they get fragile,
And they're the ones guilty of making a mess,
So fannies, I'd venture to say, are the tops,
But some of the time, they're to fear,
They're worth such a lot, but they're not quite so hot,
On thirteen occasions each calendar year.

Graham Eastaugh 25/2/99

# Lunatic fringe

I knew when I saw the Invisible Man,
That things weren't proceeding according to plan,
'Cause if he's invisible how can it be,
His presence was visibly witnessed by me?
This vision had worried me more than a tad,
It struck me I'd started to go barking mad,
My brain had been one of my last working parts,
I'd now crossed the line where insanity starts,
I started to think that EastEnders was *real,*
That Mother Teresa had huge sex appeal,
That all politicians meant all that they said,
And Colonel Gaddafi was *not* a dickhead,
I'm starting to think there's a God after all,
I've even convinced myself Bush is no fool,
The moon's made of cheese and the sun isn't hot,
And modern society's *not* gone to pot,
I'm certain the cat from next door is possessed,
I no longer want to see J-Lo undressed,
I've started believing I'll one day grow up,
I even thought England might win the World Cup,
It's no use pretending; I'm losing my mind,
I'm seeking asylum of lunatic kind,
I seem to be losing more marbles each day,
I used to shoot pool; now I'm just shot away,
I've clearly gone bonkers, yet nobody knows,
I'm scrambled inside and yet none of it shows,
Not one person's noticed my mental decline,
So maybe I've been a bit mad all the time?

Graham Eastaugh 1/7/02

# Secret affair

I'll tell you a tale from a long time ago,
A tale which, if honest, still saddens me so,
I've since changed my ways, though I still hurt inside,
So don't think this tale's one in which I take pride,
Although I was quite young, I can't be excused,
The trust of my girlfriend back then was abused,
She's no longer with me; Jeanette was her name,
I fully accept I was solely to blame,
The first time she caught me I felt such a fool,
I tried to escape by denying it all,
She'd found something odd on the seat of my car,
Some open-crotch panties and peekaboo bra,
I told her it must have been some sort of joke,
The lads from the pub or that piss-taking bloke,
Who lived down the road, and she seemed to agree,
But that's not the end of my tale, as you'll see,
A few weekends later it happened again,
The glove box this time was the cause of my pain,
She found a suspender belt; stockings as well,
A gift for her birthday's the lie I would tell,
Again she believed me; I'd got out of jail,
But one more mistake and our romance would fail,
This time, in the bedroom, I had to be candid,
I had to come clean 'cause she'd caught me red-handed,
The hurt in her eyes was abundantly clear,
A lump in her throat would then quickly appear,
She felt so betrayed I had morals so slack,
I'd broken her heart; she'd been stabbed in the back,
I loved her, you know, but I couldn't pretend,
I knew our affair had to come to an end,
I don't wish to sound like I'm whingeing as such,
But being a transvestite cost me so much.

Graham Eastaugh 10/11/01

# Just an illusion

Does anyone else still remember the time,
Way back in the old days before there was crime?
When people worked hard for a good, honest crust,
And neighbours existed on mutual trust?
When kids roamed the streets without fear of abuse,
And no one need worry of fiends on the loose?
When women were treated with utmost respect,
And perfect behaviour was all you'd expect?
My elders would tell me of times from the past,
How modern day morals would leave them aghast,
They spoke of an age that was simply ideal,
When no one used violence, and no one would steal,
I heard of how nobody broke any laws,
And people would sleep without locking their doors,
All children were safe, they would strongly insist,
'Cause villainous paedophiles didn't exist,
But over the years, I began to ask questions,
And started to doubt these idyllic suggestions,
The stories I'd heard were just tiny extracts,
It turns out I hadn't heard all of the facts,
I found an old diary my granddad had kept,
He wrote he'd been burgled at night while he slept,
He wanted the criminals brought to the dock,
And wished he had bothered to purchase a lock,
He wrote with disgust how a neighbour from hell,
Had grandchildren who were his children as well,
How children's complaints of abuse were absurd,
'Cause children were there to be seen, but not heard,
He spoke of some workmates with very hard lives,
Who gave a good thrashing to second-class wives,
He wrote of how people spoke only the truth,
And how there was no lead left on the church roof,
So what of these stories of halcyon years,

To which every pensioner staunchly adheres?
The passing of time can play tricks on the mind,
Whereby everything's grand once it's decades behind,
So life in the past wasn't quite as it seems,
For, as I suspected, the tales are just dreams,
But don't fault the old folk, for they're not to blame,
'Cause in a few years, we'll be saying the same.

Graham Eastaugh 25/3/99

# Damn Yankees

So there I was sat down awaiting the action,
When out of the silence came utter distraction,
American accents behind me boomed out,
And rules of accepted behaviour they'd flout,
The drama in front of me started to roll,
When one of the Yanks shouted: "Get in the hole!"
It did, and proceedings were going to plan,
Then one of his mates screamed aloud: "You're the man!"
"Go get 'em, big man!" another one yelled,
A sign with the words saying 'Quiet please' was held,
The other participant followed him in,
Then both the performers walked off with a grin,
A couple more chaps took their turn at the scene,
The lack of respect from those Yanks was obscene,
"Get in the hole! Way to go!" cried one bloke,
Precisely as one of the guys played his stroke,
By now I was livid, and blowing my top,
I turned round and told all these loudmouths to stop,
But none of them listened; they laughed in my face,
And told me to get the hell out of the place,
It's pointless to reason with drunkards I thought,
I went home dejected I'm sad to report,
My plans for the future are perfectly plain,
I won't watch an Amsterdam sex show again.

Graham Eastaugh 26/10/01

# Tales of the unexpected

"He's definitely gay," stated Tiffany's friend,
Not wishing their friendship to come to an end,
But Tiffany wouldn't accept Phoebe's view,
And said her opinion was simply untrue,
They'd both spent a night in a countryside pub,
Before moving on to a popular club,
Where Tiffany spotted the man of her dreams,
Though Phoebe informed her all's not what it seems,
The fellow in question and Tiffany met,
A few months before; now their wedding was set,
But Phoebe could hold back her secret no more,
The following story then came to the fore:
"I saw him last week in the park," Phoebe said,
"Your sweetheart was giving another man head,
They started off kissing, then Bob ventured south,
And promptly inserted his knob in his mouth,
The other chap came, and Bob swallowed the lot,
And, basically, that was the end of the plot,
You *can't* go ahead with your wedding in May,
Your husband-to-be is quite obviously gay."
But Tiffany disbelieved each single word,
And branded the whole sordid story absurd,
She shouted: "There's no way you're ruining my summer,
Remember, one swallow does *not* make a bummer."

Graham Eastaugh 25/7/07

# Zero tolerance

They sat at a table; six men from each side,
Their mission was peace, but their goal was denied,
The fact they had problems was never in doubt,
They now faced the headache of sorting them out,
Proceedings began with an air of goodwill,
And things started off looking hopeful until:
"We want back our homeland," aggressively said,
A man with a tea towel adorning his head,
The other side strongly objected to this,
And saw the demand as grotesquely amiss,
The man mediating then called for a truce,
Then someone said 'Bollocks!' and all hell let loose,
A man with a crooked nose rose to his feet,
And shouted, before he returned to his seat:
"We won't budge an inch, so don't treat us like fools,
Although we've no foreskins, we've plenty of balls."
He said it was *their* land, and theirs it would stay,
And gestured the man with the tea towel away,
A peaceful agreement was nowhere in sight,
So both sides agreed to continue the fight,
All hope for the future had ended in tears,
They went on with life like for thousands of years,
It's hard to imagine more bigoted views,
But that's what you get between Arabs and Jews.

Graham Eastaugh 1/5/01

# The best days of our lives

The Sixties were great, I'm persistently told,
That decade provided the best times of all,
Nothing compares, either modern or old,
Everyone those days was having a ball,
But surely not everyone thought they were great?
I quite understand they were grand for the young,
But what of those born at an earlier date?
Are such rave reviews commonplace in their tongue?
It must have been great being young at that time,
With all the world changing, and nothing a drag,
But not for those citizens well past their prime,
And carrying round a colostomy bag,
And this is my point; they were good for a kind,
The youth of the day had the time of their lives,
But everyone's better days stick in the mind,
And better days happen when youthfulness thrives,
The truth is all decades are top of the tree,
The way that we judge them is all down to age,
The younger we are, then the better they be,
And each generation has been all the rage,
Whatever the time, it was magic for some,
The Sixties weren't better or worse than the rest,
For some, there are great days for decades to come,
Our dates of birth tell us which ones are the best.

Graham Eastaugh 15/10/99

# Harry the hedgehog

Harry the hedgehog had fallen in love,
He'd met a young lady from heaven above,
He saw her one day on a walk in the park,
And chatted her up until well after dark,
A good-looking girl, she could hardly be better,
She dressed like a queen, and was called Henrietta,
Harry's emotions were pulled right apart,
For young Henrietta had captured his heart,
They kissed and they cuddled, and eager to please,
He walked her back home, and they even swapped fleas,
She made him a coffee, then led him upstairs,
He felt really chuffed, but was caught unawares,
He cursed as she started to fondle his portions,
For none of the hedgehogs had taken precautions,
He quickly got dressed, and departed the scene,
And looked for a pub with a condom machine,
He finally found one, but much to her fears,
He didn't come home till he'd had a few beers,
His drunken arrival created a storm,
For just when it mattered, he couldn't perform,
He put on his clothing, and said his goodbyes,
And thought how his drinking bout wasn't so wise,
His skinful of lager had turned out a drag,
By costing poor Harry a much-wanted shag,
Then on his way home, while traversing the road,
He failed to obey the revered Green Cross Code,
He walked straight ahead, but was right out of luck,
He let out a scream, and was squashed by a truck,
So, Harry, alas, paid the price of romance,
He'd given his life for a bulge in his pants,
This ode has a point, and the moral is this,
All amorous hedgehogs should stay off the piss.

Graham Eastaugh 8/5/99

# Behind the times

Technology seems to be out of control,
For everything's moving so fast on the whole,
The moment I think that I've got up-to-date,
Something new crops up to make me too late,
It seems such a mad technological race,
I can't be the only one not keeping pace,
It's progress, I know, but that's all very well,
It doesn't seem long since I learnt how to spell,
We've gadgets for this, and we've gadgets for that,
And things that we've recently bought are old hat,
We don't move a muscle, or turn a new page,
As lethargy rules in this push-button age,
Computers are more and more running the land,
And soon there'll be nothing completed by hand,
And where will it end? It's confusing my head,
We'll soon have computers to get out of bed,
The speed of it all is just blowing my mind,
The harder I try, I keep lagging behind,
Technology's fine, but I'd like now and then,
To try out my brain cells with paper and pen,
I'm so out of touch, I've been losing my way,
I feel like a man from a different day,
The world's moving so fast, I wonder if soon,
A spaceship will carry a man to the moon?

Graham Eastaugh 23/10/99

# Pride and prejudice

I'm quite patriotic; my loyalty's sworn,
I'm proud of the country in which I was born,
But one thing that makes me an unhappy chap:
The words of our national anthem are crap,
It's not my intention to sound really mean,
But why should I sing about saving the Queen?
I'm sorry to make such a terrible fuss,
But who really thinks that *she* cares about *us*?
Of course, she's quite keen we keep rolling along,
Ensuring her family's income stays strong,
But why can't we be a republic instead,
Of keeping a clan that's been mostly inbred?
But back to our anthem, does anyone else,
Object to including the Irish and Welsh?
I mean no offence, but the biggest of shocks,
Is having a tune that's part-owned by the Jocks,
We pledge our allegiance while under her reign,
We're seen as her subjects, which seems so insane,
The concept of royalty leaves me aghast,
To me, it belongs many years in the past,
The future's not rosy 'cause when her time's done,
We'll probably have to put up with her son,
It's England I'm proud of, and not those who rule,
I'm *not* asking God to save that jug-eared fool.

Graham Eastaugh 10/3/00

# War and peace

So Britain's last Tommy has drawn his last breath,
The 'war to end all wars' continues in death,
From this moment forward, to learn of that age,
The only referral's a history page,
But what have we learned from this lesson of war?
We'd certainly not taken heed from before,
And twenty-one years from the end of the First,
The Second World War staked its claim as the worst,
The truth is despite all the horror and pain,
We always set off down the same road again,
We can't break the cycle of war after peace,
They're easy to start but much harder to cease,
And what have we learned on perspective of life?
With lack of respect towards others now rife,
We've somehow lost sight of what liberty means,
Society's falling apart at the seams,
Forget the recession; that's not an excuse,
For crass exhibitions of social abuse,
The easy way out is to point to bad luck,
The modern approach to life's passing the buck,
So many gave so much so we can be free,
But so many folk seem unable to see,
That life is to cherish in so many ways,
And Britain's last Tommy is someone to praise.

Graham Eastaugh 14/8/09

# A conflict of names

"Don't be a wally," exclaimed little Dick,
Implying that Herbert was being quite thick,
But Charlie thought Dick was a tad out of line,
Insisting that Herbert's behaviour was fine,
Wally, however, thought Charlie was wrong,
Believing that Dick had been right all along,
He called him a herbert and left it at that,
But Charlie was keen on prolonging their chat,
He called him a dick, with a snarl on his face,
Quite satisfied Wally was put in his place,
Dick reckoned Charlie was being absurd,
But Herbert intended to have the last word,
He called Dick a charlie and gave him a slap,
While Wally was left in a state of mishap,
And Charlie was starting to wish he'd stayed quiet,
While Dick was considering starting a riot,
All four of them squared up prepared for a fight,
Not one of them feeling remotely contrite,
But just before anything dire went ahead,
They all hurried home to their sheilas instead.

Graham Eastaugh 6/11/09

# Lost in translation

"I say, my dear boy," said the old-fashioned gent,
"Would you care for a share of my shag?"
The person he asked didn't know what he meant,
So: "Fuck off!" said the young scallywag,
The old-fashioned gent answered: "Don't be like that,
I'm trying to give it away,
You're jolly aggressive for such a young chap,
Your life should be happy and gay."
The scallywag said: "Are you taking the piss?"
And his face was a picture of fear,
The old-fashioned gent then responded with this:
"You're looking a little bit queer,
How about coming back home to my place?
I've a farm; you can sample my plums,
I'll soon pump some colour back into your face,
And then you can meet all my chums,
We can go for a drink, bum around for a spell,
I love a good bender, you see,
We'll visit a gentlemen's club I know well,
And share a few faggots for tea."
"Fuck off, you queen!" the young scallywag shouted,
And threatened to pull out a knife,
"I wish I'd your spunk," the old-fashioned gent spouted,
Then caught the bus home to his wife.

Graham Eastaugh 14/5/01

# The power of love

"Okay," said my mate, "so she's got a fat arse,
And one of her eyeballs is made out of glass,
Her left tit's at least twice the size of the other,
And maybe she looks the same age as her mother,
She suffers from acne much more than I'd like,
And down at my local her nickname's 'The bike',
With money, it's true, she's incredibly mean,
And all her remaining teeth look rather green,
She might fart a lot, but her heart's made of gold,
She won't beat me up if I do what I'm told,
And, granted, her breath always stinks of neat gin,
But most days she shaves off the hairs on her chin,
The fact is I love her with all of my heart,
And nothing could possibly prise us apart,
Although you may think she's the wrong girl for me,
You'll just have to get used to how things will be."
I fully respected the things that he'd said,
And promised I'd put my misgivings to bed,
I stood up to leave, while admiring him so,
Then asked for my girlfriend back. He replied: "No."

Graham Eastaugh 24/6/07

# Communication breakdown

"Who was that Scotsman - a boxer called Jim,
Who won a world title, was lightweight and slim,
Who fought in the Seventies; Eighties as well?
My mind has gone blank for a momentary spell."
The man who was asked the aforementioned question,
Immediately made an assertive suggestion,
"Watt," he replied to his questioning friend,
The questioner took the stick by the wrong end,
"That boxer," he said, "what the hell was his name?
I picture his face but my memory's lame,
I can't for my life put his surname in place,
I wonder can *you* put a name to his face?"
"Watt, you daft twat!" sternly came the reply,
The questioner had a mad look in his eye,
"What did you call me?" he yelled at his mate,
The tempers of both men were not to abate,
"I called you a twat 'cause I answered you 'Watt',
One hell of a fault with your hearing you've got."
The other man said with a look of disdain,
"You answered me 'What?' so I asked you again."
The other man said: "That's the answer, you cunt,
The fact you ignored me is such an affront,
I answered you 'Watt' then you asked me once more."
But still there was further confusion in store,
"Don't call me a cunt, you belligerent fool,
I asked you a straightforward question, that's all,
I know he was Scottish and won a world belt,
But can't quite recall how his surname was spelt."
"Watt," said the other man angrily so,
The questioner said: "If you don't bloody know,
Shut the fuck up and stop acting so dense,
I'll ask someone else with a little more sense."

Graham Eastaugh 23/4/02

# Pouring scorn

It rained every day, and it rained every night,
It rained all the time, and was never once bright,
Two months it lasted; like rain from a tap,
The weather in England can really be crap,
Then out of the black came a glimmer of blue,
The rain clouds relented, and sunshine broke through,
The sun had its hat on, and came out to play,
The skyline was clear, and the rain went away,
The roads were like rivers; the fields were like lakes,
The cats were like drowned rats, and birds were like drakes,
The whole of the country was soaked to the core,
I'd never seen such a huge deluge before,
I turned on the box for a local reaction,
But quickly was driven to utter distraction,
A newscaster said that despite all the rain,
A ban on all hose pipes was starting again,
Now, what's going on? Are they taking the piss?
For no other country has trouble like this,
How can this be on an island like ours?
It rains all the time. Have we no reservoirs?
If England were ruling the whole of the globe,
I wonder what new ways of saving we'd probe?
A new way of not wasting snow would they choose?
And ban all the Eskimos building igloos?

Graham Eastaugh 4/9/99

# Pleasures of the flesh

The first time I sampled a woman's delights,
Was truly the utmost of wonderful nights,
My instincts till then hadn't been kept at bay,
But never before had I gone all the way,
She lay there beside me, the atmosphere tense,
I saw it as no time for feeble pretence,
I whispered, quite honestly, eyes to the floor,
I'd not, until now, ever done this before,
Although very nervous, I looked in her eyes,
And started to stroke her immaculate thighs,
I felt so excited, but tried to stay calm,
So switched my attention to holding her arm,
By now I was sweating; I'd started to shake,
The height of arousal I barely could take,
It's then I decided to make my first move,
For now was the time to get into the groove,
Her face was delightful; her breasts were divine,
Two youngsters together, and *she* was all mine,
Her body was gorgeous; her legs were the best,
I'm too much a gent to describe all the rest,
And that was it really; my story unfurled,
My first time had put me on top of the world,
The prison psychiatrist said I was mad,
But being a cannibal isn't so bad.

Graham Eastaugh 15/4/01

27

# Not up to scratch

I'm nobody special; an ordinary soul,
A run-of-the-mill sort of chap on the whole,
Not over-intelligent; likewise not dense,
A person of something like average sense,
So given the fact that I'm par for the course,
It's fair to assume that my view be endorsed,
By others who live on this planet like me,
That why all the cockups wherever we be?
But thinking more deeply, I now understand,
Why all the ineptitude throughout the land,
I thought of the years of my life spent at school,
And found myself making more sense of it all,
I thought of the dullard who sat to my right,
Remembered the short kid who wasn't too bright,
My memory called up the ginger-haired dunce,
Recalling a whole host of half-witted runts,
But 'Lofty' became a financial high roller,
His dunderhead mate an air traffic controller,
The carrot-topped kid's now become Chief of Police,
And one runs a charter flight daily to Greece,
Another one's earning his corn in the courts,
Another one's signing headmaster's reports,
They all seemed to be the most brainless of knobs,
Yet most ended up in responsible jobs,
And there lies the answer; wherever we go,
Then that's why there's such inefficiency so,
For while my tale's merely a fictional game,
Real life and my story are roughly the same,
Wherever life takes us, whatever the day,
There's always a halfwit obstructing our way,
Recall all the fools that you've known in your life,
And then understand why such terrible strife,
For most of these dimwits have jobs of a kind,
Regardless of content and depth of the mind,

We've so many people just drifting along,
Just being incompetent; getting things wrong,
We think we're so clever, but I'm not so sure,
With all the inadequacy we endure,
I've said it before, and I'll say it again,
We're mostly dysfunctional berks in the main.

Graham Eastaugh 3/7/01

# Is there anybody out there?

It happened at midnight some ten years ago,
It followed me home with a luminous glow,
I felt rather nervous, and started to jog,
The streets were deserted, and shrouded in fog,
And then without warning, I stopped my advance,
I froze on the spot, as if caught in a trance,
And that's when it happened. I know it sounds daft,
Some little men beamed me up into their craft,
My eyes were glazed over; my head started spinning,
I felt in a daze. This was just the beginning,
I said a quiet prayer, and prepared for my doom,
Then some beautiful women walked into the room,
One of the little men took me aside,
I thought it was curtains, and felt petrified,
He lined up the women, their backs to the wall,
And told me I had to have sex with them all,
The whole situation was so enigmatic,
And several hours later the girls were ecstatic,
It turned out the little men came here from space,
And used me to father a new master race,
The little men's leader then bade me farewell,
He beamed me to earth, and he came down as well,
I somehow lost consciousness. Then I came round,
He must have been ill. There was sick on the ground,
I'd lost all my bearings, and felt all confused,
My spaceship encounter had left me bemused,
I must have been brainwashed, then thrown to the floor,
My memory was dim, and my head really sore,
Then quick as a flash, I was left on my own,
The little man vanished. I stood there alone,
The spacecraft had gone; disappeared with the mist,
It really did happen. Or was I just pissed?

Graham Eastaugh 10/3/99

# Unknown quantities

We all have a face for the public to see,
We're none of us *quite* as presented to be,
We all have a private side hidden from view,
A side which to others would strike as untrue,
In nearly all cases the facts are benign,
The bulk of us stay the right side of the line,
But though we feel certain that something is so,
We never without any doubt *really* know,
The lawyer next door with a wife and a son,
Whose public perception is second to none,
Might harbour a shadier side to his life,
And bugger his offspring and batter his wife,
We all think we judge other people so well,
But actually no one can ever quite tell,
Exactly what somebody else is about,
There's always a certain percentage of doubt,
The frumpy old woman who doesn't say much,
Might go like a train at a gentleman's touch,
She might share her bed with a woman some nights,
Or maybe she contravenes animal rights?
The arrogant braggart with proud public face,
Just might be a borderline suicide case,
The kind, caring husband might find an escape,
In leading a double life practising rape,
We think we're in tune as to knowing what's what,
But might credit someone with something they're not,
The people we love we might actually hate,
Should someone be shielding a sinister trait,
Whatever's considered straightforward and pure,
Can never be taken for granted as sure,
Whatever the strength of a person's belief,
We're never quite certain what lurks underneath.

Graham Eastaugh 23/12/01

# Blanks for the memory

This illness of mine is destroying my brain,
My power of thought's ever more on the wane,
My memory's fading that things are so poor,
I'm not sure what's fiction or fact any more,
I'm certain the things that I know are there still,
It's just that I can't recollect them at will,
It's almost as if there's my mind and there's me,
My mind sometimes locked, and me losing the key,
I feel like a cabbage that's rotting away,
More brain cells go AWOL with each passing day,
And each time I feel at the depths of the mire,
I'm out of the frying pan into the fire,
It's hard to explain, but my head's in a mess,
I'm losing the years that I've lived, more or less,
As every day ends it's a page from the past,
A day from my childhood's as fresh as my last,
I live in a time warp; each day seems my first,
I'm so shot away, I'm not fearing the worst,
The whole of my life appears merely a dream,
A picture book fantasy trip, it would seem,
I'm finding it hard to maintain concentration,
I'm frequently driven to exasperation,
I'm not sure exactly what planet I'm on,
My one consolation is......sorry, it's gone.

Graham Eastaugh 12/4/01

# Wrap up!

I felt really bored just a few nights ago,
I picked up the phone and rang someone I know,
I asked if he wanted to go out that night,
He paused for a moment, then answered 'All right,'
We met at a pub up in London's East End,
He showed up at eight with a strange-looking friend,
I asked who he was; just a name would suffice,
His friend was a rapper named Cool Doggy Ice,
"Yo! How ya doin', my man, give me five,
When I'm on the scene all the chicks come alive,
I'm hungry for pussy; it don't matter which,
You goddamn mother-fuckin' son of a bitch!
I'm ready to groove; I'm a passion machine,
My gun's fully cocked, if ya know what I mean,
So get ready, ladies. I'm giving it big,
I'm steamin' for hot-blooded action, you dig?"
The people around us just stood and observed,
And maybe the looks we received were deserved,
I felt so embarrassed I ran for the door,
I'd never felt so bloody stupid before,
The way that some idiots talk is a joke,
It's hardly surprising the scorn they provoke,
It's sad I went home in a rush, and here's why:
I didn't hear Cool Doggy Ice's reply.

Graham Eastaugh 9/5/01

# Completing the circle

A funny thing happened on the way to the grave,
My body perplexed me by how it behaved,
I started my days with no teeth and no hair,
And largely depended on round-the-clock care,
But as I got older, I increased in strength,
And parts of my body expanded in length,
I soon had some teeth, and some hair on my head,
And then I was able to sleep in a bed,
My first year of life was extremely unhappy,
I had no control, and was wrapped in a nappy,
And when I was hungry, I used to go wild,
I felt really helpless, and screamed like a child,
I dribbled a lot, and my memory was poor,
I felt quite unsafe with my feet on the floor,
But as I grew stronger, it soon came to pass,
I learnt how to talk, and could wipe my own arse,
I slept a lot less, and was dressing myself,
My memory bank grew; I was in the best health,
My confidence soared, and I lost all my fears,
And this carried on for a number of years,
My faculties then took a turn for the worse,
Everything started to go in reverse,
I'd lived to my peak, but was starting to frown,
I had to face facts, I was on the way down,
My hair started thinning; I had fewer teeth,
My memory was fading beyond all belief,
My best days were gone, because now I felt sadder,
I'd lost all control of my bowels and my bladder,
My legs became shaky, and parts of me shrank,
My personal hygiene was such that I stank,
The dribbling came back, then I needed more sleep,
By now, I had very few memories to keep,
It's funny how life takes its course, don't you think?

The minute you think you're afloat, then you sink,
We start at the bottom, then climb to the top,
We gradually rise, and then gradually drop,
Life's just a circle, and once it's begun,
There's lots to enjoy, then it's back to square one,
The start and the end aren't the fun they might seem,
So make sure you have a good time in between.

Graham Eastaugh 31/3/99

# A bridge too far

I read in the paper a few years ago,
About a new treatment that worried me so,
Reversing the menopause; that was the news,
It filled me with all sorts of negative views,
A medical breakthrough, without any doubt,
With many a plus to be shouting about,
But one thing appalled me while scanning the page:
Extending a woman's fertility age,
Of course, this is great news for many a soul,
A modern day marvel of science, on the whole,
But think about some of the wild implications,
I can't be alone in my stark estimations,
They talk about setting up ovary banks,
A system of storage fertility tanks,
The bad thing about it, I truly believe,
Is women of pensioner age can conceive,
Offending the elderly's not my intention,
But who wants a mum who's collecting her pension?
All babies need parents who still have their youth,
Not wrinkly old grannies so long in the tooth,
But given the option, it's bound to take place:
The first over-seventy pregnancy case,
And bugger the fact our morality's frayed,
Just think of the medical progress we've made?

Graham Eastaugh 26/9/99

# Animal instincts

It takes quite a lot to surprise me these days,
I'm never a soft touch to shock or amaze,
But something I watched on the TV last night,
Did nothing but fill me with horror and fright,
A sad documentary, it has to be said,
About zoophilia bamboozled my head,
For those that don't know, I'll enlighten your minds,
It's sexual attraction to animal kinds,
I know these things happen, and have done for years,
It's just, in my mind, the thought never appears,
Never, that is, till the evening in question,
I can't understand the romantic suggestion,
There's many a weirdo in history to note,
But what sort of person would French kiss a goat?
And if someone's lover's a dog or a cow,
Is oral sex practised? And if it is, how?
I can't understand how a person gets off,
On contact with creatures that feed from a trough,
Or humping a camel, or porking a pig,
Or riding a horse till its todger grows big,
Or stuffing a turkey, or ramming a ewe,
Or goosing a chicken, or taming a shrew,
This sort of behaviour I cannot approve,
For how many animals make the first move?
But folk with pet fancies can do as they choose,
I don't give a monkey's; *I've* nothing to lose,
These 'animal lovers' can cause *me* no harm,
As long as the perverts stay home on the farm.

Graham Eastaugh 15/9/99

# Never again?

Geneticists seem to be going too far,
The door to disaster looks somewhat ajar,
For while our expansion of knowledge *seems* great,
I feel that catastrophe's lying in wait,
We'll soon have identified all of our genes,
So in the near future, we'll then have the means,
Of playing at God with our own DNA,
And breeding our offspring our own chosen way,
The plus points of this are enormous, of course,
Like ruling out serious defects at source,
But part of me's worried that won't be the case,
I fear of all sorts of misdeeds taking place,
Our knowledge, I'm sure, will be put to good use,
But surely it's open to racial abuse?
There's bound to be someone promoting the need,
For trying to raise a superior breed,
We'd love to eliminate illness and pain,
And never go back to the dark days again,
It's hard to complain at improving our health,
But history's fond of repeating itself,
I might be a cynic who can't see ahead?
My mind might be filled with unwarranted dread?
And maybe it's good to have babies designed?
The name Josef Mengele then came to mind.

Graham Eastaugh 21/1/00

# Love thy neighbour

When I was a kid, many years in the past,
I thought that forever my childhood would last,
Behaving myself seemed a bit of a drag,
I'd much rather act like a young scallywag,
I and my mates were a worrying sight,
And once on a freezing cold October night,
We all skipped our homework, and met on the street,
And called on some neighbours to play trick or treat,
The first house we came to, I knocked on the door,
A middle-aged man asked me what was it for,
I told him the reason, then gave him his choice,
He gave his reply in a serious voice,
As soon as he answered, his face became red,
'Cause one of my friends threw a brick at his head,
We smashed all his windows, and called him a twat,
We tied up his missus, and tortured his cat,
But now I'm much older, I'm full of remorse,
That kind of behaviour I'd never endorse,
I can't turn the clock back; I wish that I could,
I hope it's a fact I'm a bad egg turned good,
And though that occasion's a long way behind,
There's one thought that's always remained on my mind,
The question that most gives my conscience a prick,
Is what would have happened had he answered 'trick'?

Graham Eastaugh 21/9/99

# Lost in space

Oh, what a dickhead am I,
For my bollocks are high in the sky,
I lit a skyrocket while still in my pocket,
And each of my nuts said 'Goodbye,'
They used to be near to my penis,
But now they're both somewhere near Venus,
We once were quite close; now I'm feeling morose,
Because so much has come in between us,
I'll never get both of them back,
I'm stuck with a vacated sack,
I'm close to the edge 'cause I've lost my two veg,
And my meat has been left on its jack,
I feel like the biggest of fools,
'Cause I broke the most crucial of rules,
I'm taking the piss, but the message is this,
You should always take care of the family jewels.

Graham Eastaugh 29/8/99

# Facing the truth

Let me share with you a thought, if I may,
I wonder if others see things the same way?
While thinking of life, in a state of confusion,
I came to a rather disturbing conclusion,
My mind took a trip along memory lane,
But, sadly, my journey would cause me great pain,
I travelled through time to the date of my birth,
And tackled the question of: what's my life worth?
It seems in my lifetime, whatever my age,
I'd just left behind an embarrassing stage,
For though at the time, I believed I was cool,
The passing of time only proved me a fool,
At twenty years old, I was sharp as a tack,
But really an absolute berk, looking back,
At thirty, I knew all there was to be known,
But still was a charlie, as hindsight has shown,
At forty, my wisdom was simply supreme,
I knew everything about life it would seem,
I've now come to realise this wasn't the case,
And all those beliefs have been sunk without trace,
I'm now nearly fifty, and think I'm so shrewd,
The truth is I'm in an illusory mood,
For as I've been told by those older than I,
The process goes on till the day that we die,
Is this tale familiar, or is it just me?
But all of our lives we're a joke, but can't see,
It's only years later we notice the truth,
We're not quite so blind when we're long in the tooth,
I find it depressing that close to my death,
My thoughts about life, as I draw my last breath,
Won't be of a person who knew where it's at,
But more of an immature, stupid old twat.

Graham Eastaugh 18/9/99

41

# It ain't necessarily so

There's a saying that really gets under my skin,
You only get out of life what you put in,
There's many a time this is so, I admit,
But sometimes in life, the rule just doesn't fit,
I'll tell you a tale from a long time ago,
The evening was young; I was feeling quite low,
I thought I'd go out for a night on the town,
And drink off the feeling of being so down,
I drank a few beers, then I drank a few more,
I drank so much lager, my head became sore,
My stomach was full; I was dead on my feet,
I then made my way to get something to eat,
I went for an 'Indian'; ordered some food,
My palate developed an extra hot mood,
I asked for the spiciest dish they could make,
It turned out to be a disastrous mistake,
My goolies were steaming, my throat was on fire,
My temperature rose about ten degrees higher,
I settled the bill, and then phoned for a cab,
And started to wish that I'd had a kebab,
I woke the next morning a desperate man,
I urgently needed the lavatory pan,
I made it in time, and was greatly relieved,
The state of my guts was quite hard to believe,
They say what you put in, you're bound to get out,
It looks good on paper, without any doubt,
I peered down the toilet from where I'd just sat,
But surely to goodness, I didn't eat *that*!

Graham Eastaugh 19/9/99

# Staying alive

Alas the giant panda is facing extinction,
Its days on the planet are numbered it seems,
It's soon to be no more a beast of distinction,
But merely the subject of make-believe dreams,
But everything's not quite the way it appears,
The fate of the panda's not quite black and white,
Survival could go on for zillions of years,
If only the panda could get its act right,
The animals' diet is solely bamboo,
While they show little interest in practising sex,
Of self-preservation they haven't a clue,
So why should we care about saving their necks?
It's time they woke up to the facts of the matter,
And had a good look at the way that they live,
Their chances are slim and they won't get much fatter,
Unless they take serious action forthwith,
No wonder they feel in a state of disquiet,
And keeping the species alive is a drag,
They need to immediately vary their diet,
And somehow they'll have to be keener to shag,
Bamboo might not be in eternal supply,
So pandas should heed these invaluable tips:
Learn how to cook, and there's no reason why,
You can't have a fry-up or chicken and chips,
Pour out some wine, so that everything's fine,
For a romantic candlelit dinner,
Take a Viagra; then after you've dined,
You should find you're on to a guaranteed winner!
Alas the giant panda is dying out fast,
Its future looks terribly bleak as it stands,
The species might soon be consigned to the past,
But, frankly, its future is in its own hands.

Graham Eastaugh 18/11/09

# Wouldn't it be nice?

Wouldn't it be nice if we all lived in peace,
And all human hatred should suddenly cease?
Wouldn't it be nice if we shared all our wealth,
And all of the world could enjoy better health?
Wouldn't it be nice if we helped one another,
And did all we could to be kind to each other?
Wouldn't it be nice to abandon all greed,
And never have people surviving in need?
Wouldn't it be nice to eradicate pain,
And never have illness prevailing again?
Wouldn't it be nice if we lived and let live,
And learned that as well as take, sometimes to give?
Wouldn't it be nice if we never felt sad,
And every new day was the best that we'd had?
Wouldn't it be nice if the world were to mend,
And natural catastrophes came to an end?
Wouldn't it be nice if these things all came true,
And all days ahead we'd have nothing to rue?
Wouldn't it be nice to have peace on all fronts?
And wouldn't it be nice to stop dreaming for once?

Graham Eastaugh 3/3/00

44

# Men behaving badly

When I was much younger, I wasn't so nice,
I acted on impulse, and never thought twice,
A petulant youth, I did as I pleased,
No one could stop me; my life was a breeze,
I earned lots of money, was cocky and loud,
And used to hang out with a horrible crowd,
We'd meet now and then for some beers and a feed,
Then drive round the town at a frightening speed,
We'd do this for hours, till the timing was right,
Then abandon our cars, and look for a fight,
Tooled up for action, we hunted in packs,
We threatened the locals, and beat up some Blacks,
I feel quite ashamed to admit all this now,
Those days are long gone, I can earnestly vow,
I won't make excuses for things that I did,
But please don't forget, I was only a kid,
We'd go to a club, and then pick up some skirt,
We all treated women as though they were dirt,
We bullied all people who got in our way,
Then laughed all about it at work the next day,
But jobs weren't aplenty; you couldn't just choose,
The options were few with such tiny IQs,
We lost all respect in the eyes of our peers,
At least we weren't idle, and all had careers,
But now I'm much older, my views have all changed,
I'm no more a bigot. It's really quite strange,
The years have matured me. That's natural, of course,
But maybe it's since I resigned from the Force?

Graham Eastaugh 23/3/99

45

# Legacy

My world's mostly rain clouds and minimal sun,
My life, to be honest, is pretty much run,
My health is so poor that I'm just hanging on,
All thoughts of enjoyment are totally gone,
My body's been ravaged by illness and pain,
My organs are damaged, including my brain,
And each day that passes, the further I fall,
The truth is that these days I'm good for sod all,
But that's not to say that I'm *totally* finished,
I've one thing to do till I'm fully diminished,
Before I depart from this terminal strife,
I want to help somebody else have a life,
And that's why I've chosen to donate my parts,
When I'm done and dusted, another life starts,
My organs can still play a part in our race,
And that's why my donor card's firmly in place,
So when the time comes and my life's at an end,
The wonderful gift of survival I'll send,
I'll happily take my last drink from life's cup,
Content in the knowledge I've stitched someone up.

Graham Eastaugh 31/10/01

# Alphabetical order

I stood at the bar with a very good friend,
And had a few drinks as a means to an end,
My goal for the evening was getting well drunk,
So thirteen or more pints of lager I'd sunk,
Then just when the end of the evening was nigh,
A man marched towards me with blood pressure high,
He strongly opposed to the language I'd use,
And told me to watch all my Ps and my Qs,
I asked him politely to wander away,
As Ps and Qs aren't in the words that I say,
He angrily asked me what game I was playing,
I gave an example of what I was saying,
I told him to fuck off, and get on his bike,
My life is my own, and I'll say what I like,
I stuck up my fingers, and called him a twat,
Then asked: "Where's the Ps and the Qs in all that?"
He said rather shyly: "I see what you mean,
With no Ps or Qs, your vocabulary's clean."
"No fucking worries, you wanker," I said,
"You're hardly to blame you're a fucking knobhead,"
He said: "Let's be friends," and he held out his hand,
Abrasive encounters he just couldn't stand,
He smiled as he said he respected my front,
So I shook his hand and said: "Fuck off, you cunt!"

Graham Eastaugh 9/3/01

# Safety first

Show me the way to go home,
I'm blind and my dog appears dead,
I had a little drink about an hour ago,
Then I filled old Prince with lead,
I should have stayed put, and not moved to the States,
This wouldn't have happened at all,
American gun laws seal so many fates,
There's not even safety at school,
And back on these shores, we should stick to our guns,
We never should follow their lead,
We owe more respect to our daughters and sons,
For firearms we shouldn't have need,
And as for those folk who say: 'What about sport?'
My view on that question is this:
Would life without guns cut the quality short,
And happiness all go amiss?
A few years ago, I invented a game,
In which nuclear missiles were used,
Okay, it's a joke, but the point is the same,
The rule of good sense was abused,
If one day our country should madly change tack,
And slacken our gun laws, we'll rue it,
I'm praying our principles never slip back,
My message is simple: don't do it.

Graham Eastaugh 9/1/00

# Fatal attraction

I used to enjoy a good drink in the past,
My craving for liquid refreshment was vast,
I'd drink anything, be it spirits or beer,
I really loved drinking each day of the year,
A friend of mine took on a counselling role,
And warned me my drinking was out of control,
He issued me with a most startling prognosis,
And told me I'd suffer from liver cirrhosis,
He said I'd a problem without any doubt,
And urged me to go about sorting it out,
He said my behaviour was oafish at best,
And told me I'd better give drinking a rest,
I told him his viewpoints were those of a fool,
I didn't have problems with drinking at all,
And although it's not in my nature to boast,
I'd say I was better at drinking than most,
I'd drink every lunchtime, and drink every night,
I knew how to put away vodka all right,
So how could he say I'd a problem with drink?
My drinking was pretty impressive I think,
I drank like a fish, yet I rarely felt pissed,
So clearly a drink problem didn't exist,
I put away awesome amounts at my peak,
And now attend group meetings three times a week.

Graham Eastaugh 15/12/01

# Keeping it in the family

It came to me recently; why I don't know,
Of human behaviour that baffles me so,
How each generation hands certain things on,
The same things that made *us* feel so put upon,
I'm talking of habits; behavioural trends,
And pastimes to suit recreational ends,
The following thoughts then appeared in my mind,
Is anyone's memory jogged as designed?
As children, we all have to do as we're told,
And many years on, when we've offspring as old,
We vow our devotion, and love undisguised,
Then urge them to do all the things *we* despised,
Do Brownies or Girl Guides, or Cubs ring a bell?
Or Boy Scouts, or maybe a choir for a spell?
Or what about Sunday School; music for some?
Or sporting involvement completely humdrum?
I'm not sure the thinking is conscious or not,
But maybe we're proving the power we've got?
A process of thought that what *we* had to do,
However we hated it, *they* should do too,
My train of thought then switched to sexual abuse,
And violence at home of inordinate use,
The answer was staring me straight in the face,
Our elders don't perish; we just take their place,
The future of mankind is lying within,
So all will be fine if we're kind to our kin,
But look all around you, and if you're like me,
A prosperous future's the last thing you'll see.

Graham Eastaugh 2/3/00

# Honesty and lies

"Be honest," she said as she stood by the bed,
"But how do I look in this dress?
I've a meeting next week, and I'd like to look sleek,
As I desperately want to impress."
I responded: "Okay," and had no more to say,
But she pressed me to say a bit more,
I said: "You look fine, absolutely divine,"
But she asked me again: "Are you sure?"
"Of course," I replied, "Are you saying I lied?"
And she said: "I just need to know,
Just say what you think; I won't kick up a stink,"
So I then went and answered her so:
"Well, the hemline's too high; much too close to the sky,
You've a fair chance of getting arrested,
It's a very low cut, and it shows off your gut,
And it highlights the fact you're flat-chested,
Your bum's looking big; you could do with a wig,
And your legs look a little bit fat,
Your face appears chubby; your stomach quite tubby,
But everything's perfect aside from all that."
She'd heard quite enough, and stormed off in a huff,
I told her to stop being silly,
"You asked for the truth, so don't go through the roof,"
Then she threatened to cut off my willy,
I ran for my life; she's no longer my wife,
Her rage was beyond my belief,
I'd said something amiss, and the moral is this:
That sometimes it's better to lie through your teeth.

Graham Eastaugh 19/5/01

# Losing the plot

I hate reading poetry written by fools,
By people too daft to adhere to the rules,
Of strictly avoiding the cardinal crime,
Of finishing lines in irrelevant rhyme,
I'm talking of people who dabble in verse,
Who finish their lines off for better or worse,
They don't give a toss if their poetry's lame,
As long as each line ends up sounding the same,
Like people who write about Azerbaijanis,
Then write the next line about cucumber sarnies,
They don't give a monkey's their poetry's shit,
As long as each ending's a suitable fit,
Like people who talk about being superb,
Then finish the next line with any old blurb,
They don't seem to care that their wording's so poor,
As long as each line sounds the same as before,
They might write an ode about Michael Schumacher,
Then go on to talk about wearing hair lacquer,
They seem unconcerned that their words are inane,
As long as each line's the same ending again,
I'm not in that mould I'm delighted to say,
I'd never take liberties rhyming that way,
The fact is my writing is simply fantastic,
I once knew a girl with loose knicker-elastic.

                                    Graham Eastaugh 12/5/01

# The mystery of words

Bad language. What is it? I'm not really sure,
A misuse of words? Or some speech that's impure?
And if it's the latter, who makes the decision,
What words be the subject of people's derision?
How is it that some words are said without blame,
While others that mean the same thing are with shame?
Whatever's becoming of freedom of choice?
I don't need a guideline to use my own voice,
While crass euphemisms are viewed in good taste,
A person who swears is considered disgraced,
But why should this be? The whole thing's absurd,
When all's said and done, a word's just a word,
Why is it wrong to say *piss,* but not *pee?*
And what's wrong with *shit* is a mystery to me,
*Pooh* is deemed fine, though it means the same thing,
And *arsehole*'s taboo, but it's fair to say *ring,*
*Willy*'s okay, but it's bad to say *cock,*
And if we say *cunt* we get greeted with shock,
Why should it be? 1 can't understand that,
When it's widely accepted to use the word *twat,*
We can't mention *bollocks,* just say *down below,*
We always mean *suck,* but we mostly say *blow,*
And why's *come* all right, although *spunk* brings a frown?
Why's *oral sex* tacky, but not *going down?*
The wrong time of month? Or a period's due?
Why we can't say it straight I haven't a clue,
We can't speak of Aids, 'cause it's bad for our health,
You can't have a *wank,* but can *play with yourself,*
But why all this hiding behind a smoke screen?
Why don't we just say the things that we mean?
Explicit expressions I simply won't duck,
Some might not like it. But who gives a fuck!

Graham Eastaugh 1/12/98

53

# A different life

Although I knew the time would come,
When thunderclouds eclipsed the sun,
When even memories disappeared,
When bad things happened like I'd feared,
I still was taken by surprise,
As logic told deceitful lies,
For nature took a frightful twist,
And gave me things that *can't* exist,
But, as I've found, they surely do,
Yet still my whole life seems untrue,
My heart has gone; my soul as well,
There's nothing left except a shell,
And how the hell can I explain,
To help another sense my pain,
The way I feel for more to share,
When living life beyond compare?
And how frustrating can it be,
That all around me cannot see,
The things I've learned throughout my fate,
The things we only learn too late,
Alas, that's life, our lessons learned,
Can't be bequeathed, but only earned,
And every hour my sorrow grows,
But that's the way the story goes.

Graham Eastaugh 18/11/01

# Only the lonely

I'd heard all about it a few months gone by,
And now I decided to give it a try,
I'd heard that involvement was virtually real,
The closest to actual sex one could feel,
To follow this sexual intention of mine,
I bought a PC and went promptly on line,
I did all the crucial electrical checks,
And got myself set for some internet sex,
I logged myself on to a Holland-based site,
And hoped to be entertained right through the night,
The girl on the screen took off all of her clothes,
And waited to act out whatever I chose,
Her body contorted in every which way,
She took on each pose I'd suggestively say,
I loosened my tie I was feeling so hot,
As Gertrude displayed all the talent she'd got,
Vibrators and dildos - she didn't hold back,
At one point she brought on an asthma attack,
But though everything was proceeding as planned,
I still ended up with my knob in my hand,
I virtually had sex with Gertrude, you see,
She virtually shared the same bedroom as me,
I virtually gave her pert bottom a spank,
And virtually ended up having a wank.

Graham Eastaugh 14/12/01

# Dazed and confused

"I've just seen some mongeese," the little girl said,
"Some mon*gooses*, sweetheart," her mother replied,
The little girl, puzzled, was scratching her head,
"But, surely, it's mongeese?" the little girl cried,
"It's mongooses, sweetheart. It's plural, you see,"
The mother instructed her baffled young child,
"I'm older than you, so just take it from me,"
The mother went on, then her daughter went wild,
The little girl screamed: "But a goose becomes geese,
Whenever the number is higher than one,
So how can a mongoose's number increase,
Without an identical rule being done?"
"It's not *being done,* it's *applying,*" said mum,
"Your grammar, quite frankly, is terribly poor,"
The little girl wept and said: "Mummy, how come?"
The mother then banged the child's head on the floor,
"It's just how it is," the mum shouted aloud,
"And, anyway, most people's grammar is shite,
So, speaking like that you'll blend in with the crowd,
Now, see if the cat caught some mouses last night."

Graham Eastaugh 1/11/01

# Men only

Some feminists get on my tits now and then,
Demanding they're treated the same as us men,
They're simply not happy just burning their bras,
They want to be spacemen on missions to Mars,
The days of the girlie are well in decline,
They want to be fighting wars on the front line,
They're fed up of sexist derogatory jokes,
They want to be boxers and priests like us blokes,
They're bored with young babies asleep in their laps,
They want opportunities just like us chaps,
They want to man spaceships that fly to the moon,
They'll want to be registered sperm donors soon!
I'm not saying women are not worth their salt,
The fact men are stronger is nobody's fault,
Say what you like, but when all goes to plan,
A woman's a woman; a man is a man,
So come on, you ladies, it's time to relax,
It's not a disgrace to bow down to the facts,
You can't alter nature, so wind in your necks,
And just face the fact you're the much weaker sex.

Graham Eastaugh 27/4/01

# Wonders of the world

What an amazing thing planet Earth is,
The thought of it all puts my mind in a tizz,
We all know its make-up, its shape and its size,
But how many know all the wherefores and whys?
I know we're suspended somewhere in the sky,
But what stops us falling? I've never known why,
I know about gravity circling around,
But can't explain how we've our feet on the ground,
I know we revolve at considerable speed,
So why we feel motionless stumps me indeed,
I know we experience different seasons,
But can't for the life of me spell out the reasons,
I know that there's weightlessness out there in space,
But can't understand how the moon stays in place,
We're ninety-three million miles from the sun,
But how it was measured I don't know, for one,
I know it's been said we're four billion years old,
But how would we know if we hadn't been told?
I know that the planet is boiling inside,
So how come it's quite often freezing *outside*?
It's then that my worldly conclusion unfurled:
We all live our lives in our own little world,
But one thought appeared in my mind above all,
That most of us understand nothing at all.

Graham Eastaugh 22/2/00

# Lost for words

"Guten morgen," said Wilhelm; "Bonjour," said Michel,
"Ciao," said Roberto; "Hola," said Manuel,
What were they on about? John didn't know,
Then everything changed, when Bjorn said: "Hello,"
The British abroad can be desperately sad,
Our linguistic knowledge is, generally, bad,
In fact, to say bad is a trifle absurd,
For, other than English, we can't speak a word,
Learning a language is just too much fuss,
*They* have to learn English to waffle with us,
If they shared *our* attitude, what would we do?
We'd travel abroad, and we'd not have a clue,
We'd dabble in sign language - argue a lot,
Then show them what jolly hard fists we had got,
But just to allay any Britisher's fears,
We'd just about manage to order some beers,
But saddest of all, our own diction's so poor,
The best English speech isn't ours any more,
For most Europeans, the old and the young,
Speak better than us when they talk in our tongue,
It's said, in the future, simplicity's planned,
American English will cover the land,
But none of *us* should get excited too much,
By that time, we'll probably talk double Dutch.

Graham Eastaugh 12/9/99

# Not in front of the children

A long time ago in my formative days,
I went through this horrible insecure phase,
I wanted for nothing wherever I went,
But had no idea of what some people meant,
I frequently found myself quite unamused,
For adults used language that left me confused,
I thought basic English I knew all about,
But listening to grown-ups would fill me with doubt,
Talking in riddles would most often govern,
I heard of a girl with a 'bun in the oven',
Not one single person would utter her name,
I just overheard she was still 'on the game',
I asked lots of questions, but no one would say,
I just heard the words 'in the family way',
Whatever was spoken, I hadn't a clue,
I felt really thick, with my head in a stew,
Then somebody mentioned a 'back alley job',
He said it was best, but would cost a few bob,
This person was safe, and would not make a sound,
And no one would know she'd been 'sleeping around',
She woke up one morning, not feeling too great,
It then came to light when 'her monthly' was late,
I finally twigged; how naive I had been,
But why all that hush for a girl's magazine?

Graham Eastaugh 13/10/99

60

# It's a log's life

I'm not very happy; my life's such a bore,
It hardly seems worth going on any more,
I've lost my direction; each day is the same,
I don't have a future, or even a name,
No one around understands how I feel,
How nature has given me such a raw deal,
The truth is I'm not quite to everyone's taste,
'Cause I'm a discharged lump of bodily waste,
I started my days in a bag called a bowel,
I had loads of mates, but the odour was foul,
Conditions were crap, though I slept like a log,
Till one day I slipped and fell into the bog,
My chance of survival seemed terribly slim,
For no one had bothered to teach me to swim,
But after a perilous trip round the bend,
I finally came to my long journey's end,
A hole in the pipe let me out on the street,
I dreamt about all the new friends I might meet,
The future looked bright; I had nothing to fear,
Then slowly, but surely, the truth became clear,
Society wanted me out of the way,
Everyone everywhere kept me at bay,
I felt so alone 'cause my face didn't fit,
To be more precise, I was treated like shit,
I'm really unhappy; I frequently sob,
I've GCSEs, but I can't get a job,
I can't get a girlfriend; I'm left on the shelf,
Flies think I'm great. Why can't anyone else?
I can't carry on; my existence is hell,
I'm treated as though I were just a bad smell,
Nobody stops in the street for a chat,
By people's reactions you'd think I'd just shat,
Every so often I'll let off a whiff,

And hope that a passing dog stops for a sniff,
But nobody loves me; I've done all I can,
I'm only at home in a lavatory pan,
So what of tomorrow? My prospects are bleak,
I'm left with no paddle, while stuck up the creek,
The world is no place for a turd of my kind,
I'm better off living up someone's behind.

Graham Eastaugh 15/11/98

# Déjà vu

If there *is* such a thing as reincarnation,
To what sort of world can I hope to come back?
Will life be the same? For in my estimation,
Whatever the era, things never change tack,
I'm sure I'll return to a world full of war,
A climate change treaty that's still unresolved,
And Arabs and Jews will be settling a score,
A land without racism won't have evolved,
With too many people existing on greed,
There'll always be others surviving on hope,
To deaf ears the poor of the planet will plead,
A prosperous future will be out of scope,
In reincarnation I've never believed,
I'd hate to come back to this mess that we're in,
So if I've been wrong, I'd be greatly aggrieved,
To do it again in a different skin,
My life's been okay, but one life is enough,
I've had a few problems concerning my health,
So if there's an afterlife, that would be tough,
And knowing my luck, I'll come back as myself.

Graham Eastaugh 22/10/99

# Pants

Lots of things change as the years travel by,
Whatever's demanded, we try to supply,
But one thing I've noticed, for better or not,
The size of our underwear's shrunk such a lot,
My dear old great granny would turn in her grave,
At thinking of how modern youngsters behave,
By walking in public with thigh muscles bare,
And sunbathing topless for all eyes to share,
Back in her day, it was bloomers and long johns,
Nothing was worn to induce sexual turn-ons,
Their underclothes often formed multiple layers,
They had more protection than ice hockey players!
A whole range of extra large garments was worn,
A bare knee on show was considered as porn,
Whatever your sex, you'd the same circumstance,
You spent all your lifetime in long, baggy pants,
But over the years, fashion had a rethink,
The size of our underwear started to shrink,
The shrinking went on, till the time's come along,
You're now overdressed if you're wearing a thong,
And what will the next change in underwear bring?
A world full of people with drawers made of string?
I don't know the answer, but one thing I know,
Life must have been nothing but pants long ago.

Graham Eastaugh 28/1/00

# Something better change

Think of what goes into making a man,
From birth to deployment in Afghanistan,
Face up to the facts if your mind will allow,
And see if you feel quite the same way as now,
All newly-born babies need round-the-clock care,
With utter devotion and loving to spare,
And so it goes on for a number of years,
As, slowly, increased independence appears,
We nurture; we cherish; we teach right from wrong,
Till one day their schooling days' end comes along,
They each have their various futures in store,
While some face the prospect of marching to war,
We're told that Afghanistan harbours a threat,
To Britain's security needs being met,
But is this a fact or a Government lie?
And, if it is, why can't we give peace a try?
It seems our endeavours are hitting the rocks,
While too many young men come home in a box,
You can't sway opinion with missiles and guns,
They might not be yours, but they're *somebody's* sons,
So much is invested in raising a child,
And so much is staked when a soldier is styled,
One life means much more than a few words can say,
It seems such a crime to just throw it away.

Graham Eastaugh 18/9/09

# As the actress said to the bishop

I went to a party a few weeks ago,
A small social gathering of people I know,
But some of the guests I'd not previously met,
I wasn't to know how quick-witted they'd get,
Out of my depth, I just stood and observed,
And lapped up the brilliant humour they served,
But judge for yourself; I'd be only too glad,
To share with you some of the laughter I had,
I walked through the door and was soon introduced,
To someone whose every word quickly induced,
So much amusement; it's hard to explain,
I'll try to relive all the humour again,
I said: "Who's that lady?" And sharp as a knife,
He said: "That's no lady, mate . . . that's my wife!"
Creased up with laughter, I struggled for breath,
It felt at the time I was laughing to death,
We talked about children; he said they had none,
He said he quite liked them . . . he used to be one,
By now I'm in stitches; my sides really ached,
I wasn't sure how much more fun I could take,
Then in walked a big-breasted girl to the sound,
Of: "You don't get many of those to the pound!"
By now I'm in tears; I was laughing so much,
I couldn't keep up; I began to lose touch,
Then somebody belched, and it couldn't be quicker,
A wag in the kitchen screamed: "More tea, vicar?"
I'm now in hysterics; I had to get out,
I'd never heard so much good humour about,
I murmured: "Excuse me." Then came the reply,
"Why, what have you done?" And I started to cry,
Never before had I had such a laugh,
I'd never heard things quite so funny by half,
So when I went home to the warmth of my bed,
I couldn't get rid of those jokes from my head,
It just goes to prove there's no truth in the rumour,
That gone are the days of original humour.

Graham Eastaugh 16/2/99

# A likely story

The young woman opened the studio door,
The man took her coat and said: "Sit on the bed."
A modelling assignment was what it was for,
"Before we begin, I've some questions," she said,
She wanted to check it was all in good taste,
And all the requirements were well above board,
On nothing indecent her CV was based,
He told her: "It's all in good taste, rest assured,
The photos I take you could show to your dad,
My focus is mainly a beautiful face,
So less of those distasteful fears that you had,
And let's get this photograph shoot taking place."
He picked up his camera and went on to say,
He travelled all over the world in his job,
He'd worked with some beautiful girls in his day,
And said: "In this game you can earn a few bob."
He told her he wanted her flat on her back,
And said he'd just come home from filming in Ghana,
He said: "Take your clothes off, and try to relax,
And act like a slag with this plastic banana."

Graham Eastaugh 8/11/01

# Animal crackers

We humans can be very fickle of mind,
In how we treat others of animal kind,
To some we're protective, but others not so,
Our attitudes differ, but why I don't know,
Our discrimination I can't understand,
The way we view creatures all over the land,
Some we're quite fond of, but others we're not,
And some get protection, while others get shot,
We always treat tigers with consummate care,
But isn't our bias towards them unfair?
We fight to preserve them, but why all the fuss?
My question is this: do they care about us?
If the roles were reversed, and *our* numbers were few,
What do you reckon the tigers would do?
Keep us from danger, and let us roam free?
Or tell us to shove it, then eat us for tea?
Rats, on the other hand, don't fare so well,
We treat them like unwelcome rodents from hell,
For, unlike the tigers, they get a bum rap,
They get no protection; just caught in a trap,
We vilify some, but on others we dote,
But shouldn't all animals share the same boat?
They all should be equal; no preference shown,
And shouldn't we humans just leave well alone?

Graham Eastaugh 20/10/99

# Strangers in the night

If ghosts really *do* exist, why's there no proof?
And why do they choose to remain so aloof?
Just one photograph, or some footage will do,
To start me believing these stories are true,
With so many people who claim to have sighted,
A strange apparition who'd been uninvited,
A logical thinker would surely surmise,
There has to be something, they can't all be lies?
But personally speaking, I need a bit more,
Than mere anecdotal reports to be sure,
If things that go bump in the night are about,
It's hard proof I need to remove any doubt,
Though having said that, there's been many a case,
When proof of existence was almost in place,
But just at the moment it seemed to be proved,
The 'facts' I demanded were cruelly removed,
I once had a friend who would strongly insist,
His presence to phantoms was hard to resist,
Wherever he went, a foul smell would appear,
It turned out he'd not had a bath for a year!
Of curtains that moved in the night he had spoken,
Forgetting to mention his windows were broken!
He also informed me of visions he'd had,
That happened before he was certified mad!
My quest for an answer was back to square one,
I desperately wanted some proof, but had none,
So if you're a ghost, I've an urgent appeal,
Stop pissing about, and just *prove* that you're real!

Graham Eastaugh 18/3/00

# The scales of injustice

Our idea of justice has reached a new low,
The Jocks have put on a contemptible show,
They've madly succumbed to a Libyan plea,
By letting the Lockerbie bomber walk free,
It's not just the Lockerbie case that's a farce,
It's many a lenient sentence courts pass,
No wonder society's living in dread,
Our judicial system's gone soft in the head,
Whatever became of those halcyon days,
When villains were punished in barbarous ways?
Like ripping their guts out or hanging 'em high,
Or drowning a 'witch' without chance of reply,
Our thieves would be packed off Australia-bound,
All murderers ended up deep underground,
All felons were faced with a judgement from hell,
And even small kids drew the short straw as well,
Those times were a little too harsh I admit,
We needed to tone down our laws just a bit,
As every year passes we lower the bar,
The trouble is, now, we've gone too bloody far!
The pendulum's swung from extreme to extreme,
The *victims* are punished these days it would seem,
I'm certain most folk would agree with this rhyme,
And just want the punishment fitting the crime.

Graham Eastaugh 25/8/09

# Love don't live here any more

"Last but not least," said the beauty to the beast,
"The love I once had for you, sadly, has ceased,
It's not just the snoring or farting in bed,
The pig-ugly face that's attached to your head,
Not even the fact that you spit when you talk,
Nor falling asleep now and then when we pork,
I'm not even bothered the toilet gets missed,
On nights you come home from the pub really pissed,
The truth is we've nothing in common at all,
What you see as hot is what I see as cool,
You love watching football, while I hate the game,
You've never been wrong, while I'm *always* to blame,
You never remember significant dates,
You think less of me than you do of your mates,
You've no personality; interests too,
You don't give a toss about things that *I* do,
It's not that your family *never* liked me,
Or even the fact that we never agree,
It's not that your personal hygiene's so poor,
Or even we rarely have sex any more,
The fact is that after our hormones cooled down,
There wasn't much left worth our hanging around."
This story I've written is fiction, of course,
But *that's* why there's such a high rate of divorce.

Graham Eastaugh 26/4/01

# Blending in with the locals

There's a theory in life that wherever you go,
The longer you stay there, you'll pick up the lingo,
But that's not for me; I won't follow the trend,
I've just spent some time up in London's East End,
I stayed with a friend and his trouble and strife,
And sampled the way of a Londoner's life,
Soon after I got there, we took in a club,
But first had some drinks at a quiet rub-a-dub,
We jumped in his jam jar, and drove down the frog,
Then ordered a cab on the bar's public dog,
I wore my best whistle, and looked really ace,
I tidied my barnet, and had a good brace,
We got to the club, and I took off my coat,
I spotted this bird with a beautiful boat,
She had gorgeous bristols; I soon made a pass,
She had such a wonderful bottle and glass,
My mate had a butcher's, and said: "Use your loaf,
She's hanging around with that big, hairy oaf."
I'd had a few sherbets, and brave as a lion,
I threatened her boyfriend, and called him an iron,
But sadly for me, my bluff didn't work,
He flew off the handle, and called me a berk,
I got really scared 'cause he had loads of mates,
I looked for the door, and was quick on my plates,
By the time I got home, it was ever so late,
I came through the door in a right two and eight,
So Brahms and Liszt, I was caught unawares,
And honked up my guts on the apples and pears,
But just 'cause I spent a few weeks in the Smoke,
I won't begin talking like some Cockney bloke,
I can't help believing this theory's baloney,
And think I've just proved it's a load of old pony.

Graham Eastaugh 15/3/99

# So help me God

The stress I'd been under was ruining my health,
I needed to get a firm grip of myself,
The pressure was too much to bear on my own,
My problems were too great to tackle alone,
I desperately needed a most special friend,
To help bring my feelings of stress to an end,
You might find the way I approached things quite odd,
But everything changed when I turned to my god,
I felt he was with me wherever I went,
My god, in a strange way, appeared heaven sent,
It all sounds a little suspicious I know,
My god was beside me wherever I'd go,
And after a while, I was less of a mess,
My god with each day was relieving my stress,
I felt a bit better with each passing day,
My god helped me bury my troubles away,
And while many folk thought it bonkers at first,
They saw me as merely eccentric at worst,
The way I approached things did nobody harm,
My god was the reason I found inner calm,
So, as a reward, a big bone I then bought,
For Fido my god, I'm so pleased to report,
I'd faced all the trauma my mind would allow,
I just need to cure my dyslexia now.

Graham Eastaugh 21/5/02

# X-rated viewing

For as long as my memory goes back in time,
I've gone from ridiculous thoughts to sublime,
I've thought of the present, the future and past,
All subjects explored from the first to the last,
But most of my thinking was pie in the sky,
Inventions I'd dreamt up, but didn't know why,
But one of my brainwaves had worked like a dream,
However, the benefits weren't as they'd seem,
I thought my invention would brighten my days,
And satisfy some of my curious ways,
If honest, I'd say I was driven by sex,
And that's how I came to invent x-ray specs,
Whenever I wore them I'd see to the skin,
All clothes were invisible focusing in,
But things didn't work out the way that I'd thought,
And some things I saw weren't the things that I'd sought,
The sight of old grannies unclad was the pits,
And so many women had unsightly tits,
To see something tasty I'd sometimes walk miles,
The girl at the fish shop I'd fancied had piles,
I saw very little to meet my desires,
Apparently slim girls were hiding spare tyres,
A few open-leg sightings made my blood curdle,
And how many beer guts were strapped in a girdle!
My specs made me sick at the end of the day,
I made the decision to throw them away,
I reached the conclusion that clothes aren't so bad,
The fact that we wear them should make us feel glad,
For some of the things that I saw were obscene,
Just look all around and you'll know what I mean,
Although this was long ago, still I can't sleep,
And who says that beauty is only skin deep?

Graham Eastaugh 9/7/01

74

# Costume drama

That fancy dress party was such a good night,
Everyone there was as high as a kite,
All kinds of high jinks for the night were in store,
Bar takings were higher than ever before,
A bloke dressed as Batman was looking my way,
Who struggled to keep his amusement at bay,
He signalled me over, so over I went,
A jolly good time in his company I spent,
I met with his wife, who was dressed as a nun,
The get-up I wore was provoking much fun,
The pair of them couldn't stop laughing at me,
They couldn't believe what a joker I'd be,
"You look like a tosser," the husband observed,
He told me the stick I received was deserved,
He gave a chap near him a tap on the head,
Then: "Look at the state of this wanker!" he said,
And so it went on with each person I met,
That evening was one I shall never forget,
It gave me a buzz to provide so much joy,
With all that attention I felt rather coy,
I finally left having been such a hoot,
And others enjoyed my appearance to boot,
There's only one drawback to cause me despair,
I'd only called in there to pick up a fare.

Graham Eastaugh 18/1/02

# Private practice

When I was much younger, aged twelve or thirteen,
One hobby I practised was mostly unseen,
I'd sit in my bedroom each night all alone,
The technical skills of my hobby I'd hone,
Then one night while taking a stroll past my door,
My mum smelt an odour she'd witnessed before,
She came in and wore a shocked look on her face,
And told me my head should be hung in disgrace,
"If you keep doing that you'll go blind," she forewarned,
Until then the risk to my health hadn't dawned,
I stopped as I spoke, then defended my deeds,
Explaining they satisfied some of my needs,
"But Mother," I said, "there's no reason for grief,
My hobby can bring me enormous relief,
I know it can smell, but you shouldn't feel stress,
Whenever I'm finished I clean up the mess."
She answered: "I'm wiser than you, you might find,
So keep doing that and I swear you'll go blind,
You shouldn't be bringing such risk on yourself,
You're not getting out and it's bad for your health."
My goggles were fine but they didn't quite fit,
I thus sold my DIY home-welding kit,
My mum said to find a new hobby instead,
"Why don't you try masturbating?" she said.

Graham Eastaugh 7/5/02

# With immediate effect

The world we all live in is changing so fast,
With very few things of today like the past,
Our manner of living has clearly moved on,
The days of tranquillity obviously gone,
Our urge for immediacy dominates all,
The days of more patience have gone to the wall,
Whatever's demanded, it has to be *now,*
Delayed interaction we just won't allow,
We nowadays don't have a second to waste,
The essence of speed is to everyone's taste,
Electronic messaging saves so much time,
And traffic delays can evolve into crime,
We've all got computer mice handy to click,
Whatever's requested, it has to be quick,
We're in such a rush for the food we devour,
And sex on a first date within half an hour,
Kids want to be old when they're patently young,
Prepubescent boys want to be better hung,
And girls of identical age are the same,
They can't wait to get a first shag to their name,
But like it or lump it 'cause that's how it is,
And if there's a God, the decision is His,
Our urge for immediacy grows ever stronger,
So how can Test cricket continue much longer?

Graham Eastaugh 28/7/01

# A night to remember

While lying in bed just the night before last,
I couldn't help thinking of days from the past,
My first day at school, and then joining the Cubs,
My first day at work, and then discos and clubs,
And that's where my story of romance begins,
A nightclub, a female, and too many gins,
For that was the time when I first fell in love,
I'd just met a girl sent from heaven above,
Or that's how it seemed when our eyes had first met,
It just goes to show you how wrong I could get,
'Cause 'Norma' was not quite the woman I'd sought,
She wasn't exactly the beauty I'd thought,
The lights had been dim, and I'd drunk quite a lot,
I wasn't sure whether I'd pulled her or not,
But when the night ended she followed me home,
She came in for coffee; we sat there alone,
I went to the bathroom; she went on ahead,
And soon we were naked together in bed,
She didn't appear the most thoughtful of lovers,
Farting in bed and then flapping the covers,
I soon realised she was lacking in class,
When catching a glimpse of her teeth in a glass,
I wanted to please her, and gave it my best,
And wasn't put off by the hairs on her chest,
She asked to do anal; I told her I would,
As Friday nights went, this had been rather good,
I felt in a dream; it was love at first sight,
But everything drastically changed overnight,
She looked really gorgeous the first time we spoke,
And she said she'd never met such a nice bloke,
But come the next day I could feel my heart crash,
On Saturday morning she'd grown a moustache!
The evil of drink is a terrible thing,
I'm tangible proof of the pain it can bring,
There's one crucial lesson I've learnt from this mess,
That's never go home with a bloke in a dress.

Graham Eastaugh 31/1/99

# A bone to pick

Religion and God have no meaning to me,
I only believe in the things I can see,
I might be mistaken I fully accept,
So where there's no proof, I've an open mind kept,
Of meeting one's Maker we've all heard it said,
On crossing the line between living and dead,
And if that's a fact, as religion reports,
I'll have to remember the following thoughts:
I'll try to be civil on meeting my death,
But not too long after I've had my last breath,
I'll collar my Maker, then take him to task,
The following questions I'll angrily ask:
Why so bad looking? And why the big nose?
And why all that acne to add to my woes?
And why so much bone? Did you run out of meat?
And what's going on with these bloody great feet?
Couldn't you make me a little bit stronger?
And why wasn't *this* made a little bit longer?
And why am I so short of cells of the brain?
And couldn't you give me less haemorrhoid pain?
And what's the big joke with this eyesight of mine?
Were all these things done by mistake or design?
And why did you give me a breakable heart?
And why did you make me a boring old fart?
Whenever my days in this lifetime are through,
There's one thing for certain I'm dying to do,
As soon as I've found me a bed for the night,
I'll say a few things to my Maker all right.

Graham Eastaugh 3/6/01

# Who'd be a turkey at Christmas?

Well, bugger me backwards, it's Christmas at last,
But I'm not at all sure I can stand it,
I'm fully prepared for my Yuletide repast,
But it's not quite the way that I planned it,
'Cause, alas, when the time comes and dinner is served,
I won't be a picture of glee,
For I've just heard the news, and have I got the blues,
'Cause I've found out the main course is *me*!
You can call me naive, but I never believed,
When they fed me all year like a king,
I was primed for a snack; now I'm so bloody fat,
That I can't see my own dangly thing,
I'm all in a stew, 'cause I've nothing to do,
Except wait for a painful demise,
When it's off with my head, then my feathers all shed,
I'll be packaged and weighed up for size,
I'll be frozen, then thawed, and then off my feet sawed,
I really won't know where I'm at,
My innards, by heck, will be paired with my neck,
And then fed to the neighbour's pet cat,
There'll be stuffing prepared in a baking tin squared,
My chances of dignity sparse,
Because flat on my back so, they'll spoon out the Paxo,
And shove the whole lot up my arse,
I'll be stuck in a stove till I'm cooked and, by Jove!
My legs will be taken by force,
My flesh will be sliced with a huge carving knife,
And then covered with cranberry sauce,
And just when it looks like my ordeal is through,
I'll be filling up sarnies for tea,
Then prepared for a feast, for the next month at least,
I'll be served up as soup for a family of three,
So think of my plight, as you bed down at night,
On the eve of your Christmas Day meal,
Picture yourself in a fridge, on a shelf,
And you might understand how I feel,

I'm as grumpy as sin because time's closing in,
So forgive me for not being perky,
But Christmas has come, which is all right for some,
But it's no bloody fun for a turkey!

Graham Eastaugh Nov 93

# One way or another

Imagine a world with no planes in the sky,
A planet from which not one aircraft can fly,
And think of a world with no automobiles,
A land that's devoid of all motorised wheels,
Of course, it's not easy to picture the scene,
For that's not the way all our lifetimes have been,
I guess you could think you were living on Mars,
A planet that's never seen airplanes or cars,
Each journey of note would take such a long time,
Ridiculous taking the place of sublime,
We couldn't live life in the same way as now,
An absence of planes and cars wouldn't allow,
But think if all governments laid down the law,
Decreeing we'd travel by these means no more,
We'd quickly see hopes superseded by fears,
By turning the clock back one hundred-plus years,
This ode's hypothetical; purely unreal,
But if planes and cars were banned how would you feel?
And if you're opposed to these two impositions,
Then stop banging on about carbon emissions.

Graham Eastaugh 29/11/09

# A good healthy appetite

"Do you fancy a toffee?" said Rick the raccoon,
To Barney the beaver one Sunday in June,
But Barney's reply was to Rick's disbelief,
He told him that toffee was bad for his teeth,
Rick the raccoon looked a trifle bemused,
For Barney's refusal had left him confused,
He paused for a moment, collecting his thoughts,
Considering Barney to be out of sorts,
"Bad for your teeth? Are you taking the piss?"
Said Rick the raccoon; then he followed with this:
"I'm not a buffoon, so stop bullshitting me,
I've just watched you gnawing your way through a tree!"
Barney said: "Ah, but that's not the same thing,
Trees don't cause the tooth decay toffee can bring,
I'm not talking bollocks; I'm telling the truth,
That none of us beavers have got a sweet tooth."
Rick the raccoon was a picture of woe,
His goofy companion puzzled him so,
He couldn't quite see how a toffee's not good,
Yet all's hunky-dory if chewing on wood,
But think for a while, and the facts are all there,
Not one single beaver requires dental care,
The next time a trip to the dentist comes by,
You won't see a beaver, and now you know why.

Graham Eastaugh 27/7/01

# Waste not want not

I still can't believe it, yet know that it's true,
How certain things happened I haven't a clue,
The fact is they did and I can't turn back time,
I'll never return to the days of my prime,
My legs were so feeble; my movement so poor,
The state of my health was too bad to ignore,
My dignity suffered; my hygiene as well,
The rest of this story's a sad one to tell,
My plight was distressing it's perfectly clear,
I suffered a sudden attack of diarrhoea,
My toilet was too many paces ahead,
I found myself using a bucket instead,
A little while later, a neighbour called round,
A strange fascination about me he found,
He looked at my bucket of stools for the day,
Then asked my permission to take it away,
I found his request just a tiny bit weird,
But everything wasn't as daft as appeared,
It happened by accident, not by design,
But that's how the Turner Prize came to be mine.

Graham Eastaugh 2/6/02

# Looking for trouble

The anguish he felt was displayed in his eyes,
His fear of the outcome he couldn't disguise,
He'd pounded the streets in his quest for relief,
But now he would meet with a moment of grief,
His path was to cross with a mean-looking brute,
Who seemed in the mood for a drunken dispute,
"Are you looking for trouble?" he noisily slurred,
The other man couldn't believe what he'd heard,
"I am," he replied with a smile on his face,
A look of sheer horror to soon take its place,
For quick as a flash he was made to see red,
The drunkard was aiming a punch at his head,
"What are you doing?" he screamed at the man,
A punch in the head wasn't part of his plan,
The drunkard responded, his face rather glum:
"You're looking for trouble - I'm giving you some."
A policeman walked by and insisted on calm,
Revealing significant stripes on his arm,
His question was most undeniably clear,
A triple "Hello." Then: "What's going on here?"
"He's looking for trouble," the drunkard replied,
A half-empty bottle of gin by his side,
The policeman, his head shaking, answered: "I see,
You two can come down to the station with me."
The other man argued he'd done nothing wrong,
He'd only been peacefully walking along,
The drunk interrupted and shouted out: "What!
He's looking for trouble, so that's what he got."
The policeman then questioned the man: "Is this true?
Is looking for trouble a thing you would do?"
"Well...yes," said the man, and the policeman said: "Right,
I'm locking you two in the cells for the night."
The policeman was tired and went home to his wife,
The drunkard had fears he was wasting his life,
The other man seemed in a world of his own,
While Trouble the dog wandered sheepishly home.

Graham Eastaugh 15/1/02

85

# Anything goes

A few decades back in the race to the moon,
The world used to dance to a different tune,
The USSR was a foe not a friend,
American kinship was not then the trend,
They fought for supremacy travelling in space,
They staged the most fierce technological race,
In those days the pair couldn't trust one another,
They strove to be one step ahead of the other,
A rocket was sent into space in one test,
With only a monkey aboard as a guest,
And that gets me thinking of what *might* have been,
The possible outcomes that might have been seen,
What if some aliens captured the craft,
To find that by solely a monkey it's staffed?
Would monkeys be viewed with high cerebral worth?
Would *we* be considered like monkeys on Earth?
Would apes get the credit in alien eyes,
For all things where human achievement applies?
And would *we* be seen as a valueless breed,
Reared purely for usage as animal feed?
And what if the monkey took charge of the ship,
And set off on some interplanetary trip?
Then came back to Earth with some creatures from Mars,
That threatened all life on this planet of ours?
Admittedly things didn't happen that way,
But anything's possible I always say,
Whatever we think of in life to be so,
We never one hundred per cent really know,
Never say never is frequently said,
But how many people think never instead?
I've learnt many things to enlighten my brain,
The most crucial not to say never again.

Graham Eastaugh 26/11/01

86

# Too close for comfort

A long time ago, though it's hard to believe,
I wanted to be just like Christopher Reeve,
I loved all those Superman films he was in,
His fights against evil which always he'd win,
He caught speeding bullets, and had x-ray eyes,
He lived his whole life as an ace of disguise,
And over tall buildings he'd comfortably jump,
A cracker called Lois Lane sometimes he'd hump,
His hearing was so sharp it seemed heaven-sent,
He'd change in an instant to being Clark Kent,
He didn't need aircraft to put him in flight,
Although he was keen to avoid Kryptonite,
I had loads of dreams as a much younger man,
I've never been solely a Superman fan,
But though many stars were an idol to me,
It's Christopher Reeve I *most* wanted to be,
And many years on, as I feel as I do,
My dream of becoming like him has come true,
There's one painful lesson I've learned from my fate,
That sometimes a dream that comes true ain't so great.

Graham Eastaugh 31/7/01

# True colours

The noble young officer opened his heart,
Addressing the girl he so greatly adored,
He told her he couldn't bear being apart,
His inner emotions he wished to record:
"Your face is delightful, sweet angel of mine,
Your beauty is simply too much for this earth,
Each part of your wonderful self is divine,
Without you beside me my life has no worth."
He held her hand warmly and looked in her eyes,
And told her his passion for her was so strong,
He told her his love for her reached for the skies,
His lust for her no longer could he prolong,
She pressed herself close to him lovingly so,
And told him her feelings for him were the same,
However, her passion for him couldn't show,
Outlining the fact that she wasn't to blame:
"My darling, I long for your loving embrace,
But, sadly, the time of the month isn't right."
A radiant smile decorated her face,
Suggesting they just snuggle up for the night,
Despite what she'd told him, his lust couldn't wait,
The noble young officer's will wouldn't flag,
The following question he asked of his fate:
"D'you reckon your sister might fancy a shag?"

Graham Eastaugh 12/4/02

# Mistaken identity

The man in the turban looked somewhat suspicious,
A devious sort of chap rather than vicious,
He stood in the street as he stared to the skies,
An image of evil I saw in his eyes,
I ran to confront him; then asked who he was,
He told me his mates at the mosque call him Oz,
"It's him!" I concluded; then pressed home my case,
And waved an American flag in his face,
He seemed slightly flustered and anxious at first,
Then smiled as he twigged I suspected the worst,
He chuckled aloud as he begged for my pardon:
"You think I'm that arsehole, Osama bin Laden?"
I told him I did as I nodded my head,
I'd take him alive or, if necessary, dead,
I gave him a punch and a couple of kicks,
And warned him he'd better not try any tricks,
He said rather angrily: "Lay off, you ponce,
Just 'cause I'm wearing this rag round my bonce,
And just 'cause it's Allah I praise every day,
Does *not* mean a terrorist's role I would play,
I might be quite tall, with an untidy beard,
My skin might be dark, but I'm not to be feared,
I know how it is, so you're hardly to blame,
We're just like the Chinkies - we all look the same."
I felt so embarrassed; my guilt was immense,
I offered my hand as sincere recompense,
He shook my hand warmly and said not to worry,
Inviting me round to his place for a curry,
The lesson I learned is we never should rush,
Into tarring a similar group with one brush,
I'd learned that this man and myself were like brothers,
Then watched as he collected his dole like the others.

Graham Eastaugh 26/09/01

# All right for some

This chap I once knew was one hell of a guy,
Everyone loved him, no word of a lie,
The rest of the blokes around town were so full,
Of envy of him because boy, could he pull!
Wherever he went he was shagging around,
His feet hardly ever seemed near to the ground,
A female of any kind suited his need,
As long as he'd somewhere for sowing his seed,
He had all the youngsters; the older ones too,
And even the 'monster' that worked at the zoo,
He had all the fat birds; the skinny 'n' all,
He had quite a few who still hadn't left school,
The short and the lofty, he'd been everywhere,
Whoever he rogered he just didn't care,
He had a few grannies; did three in a bed,
I've never known someone with so much street cred.,
I've tried to explain things the best that I can,
But just take my word for it - *he* was the man,
A sackful of conquests was all he'd expect,
So everyone paid him enormous respect,
This bloke had a sister; in fact she's his twin,
But nobody liked her a lot, unlike him,
She spent all her life with her legs wide apart,
And had *loads* of boyfriends - the shameless old tart.

Graham Eastaugh 1/6/01

# The feminine touch

The misuse of drugs in athletics is rife,
I'm sure that's the way that it's been throughout life,
Of course, you'll find drugs used in all types of sport,
It's just that athletics sees more of them caught,
Rewards are so high, it's a practice worth chancing,
They seem worth the risk when performance enhancing,
I've always had doubts, but I couldn't be sure,
But recent events left me shocked to the core,
I watched the World Championships, broadcast from Spain,
But some of the sights caused me terrible pain,
The level of cheating was simply immense,
The worst scenes arose in the women's events,
The German shot-putter had legs like a man,
A Chinese girl's bollocks swung each time she ran,
A big, bouncing Czech woman's tits disappeared,
And one girl from Russia tripped over her beard,
It seemed like an advert for testosterone,
And one girl looked just like Sylvester Stallone,
The end of another girl's penis turned black,
And someone from Poland had hair on her back,
It must be a great feeling being the best,
To say that you're better than all of the rest,
To stand as your national flag is unfurled,
And being acclaimed as on top of the world,
But this way of winning I cannot condone,
It's best to leave natural hormones alone,
It's great to win gold, and enjoy the effects,
But not at the high price of changing your sex?

Graham Eastaugh 3/9/99

# You know what I mean?

I went to the doctor's a few days ago,
I had this incredible pain down below,
I took all my clothes off, and showed him the spot,
Where all this discomfort I'd suddenly got,
He gave me a poke, and he gave me a dig,
He had a quick look at my thingamajig,
He said it was best that he then overhaul it,
And then he examined my whatd'you-call-it,
He told me to cough; then to lie on the couch,
And then he proceeded to make me say 'Ouch!'
He wanted to know had it ever turned black,
And asked me if I could still pull the skin back,
I told him I could, but it bloody well hurt,
And sometimes a discharge would messily spurt,
I said I was fairly okay passing water,
Then thought of the presents I'd foolishly bought her,
He told me to give the old business a miss,
For three or four weeks; then he came up with this:
He said should I manage the odd resurrection,
Be sure to be armed with some foolproof protection,
And that was it really; he gave me some pills,
And seemed pretty certain they'd cure all my ills,
In most graphic detail I've painted the scene,
I'm now off the booze, if you know what I mean?

Graham Eastaugh 2/6/01

# Slang evolution

It's funny how certain words drift out of fashion,
Especially those that interpret our passion,
Like *bonk*, for example, which gave way to *shag*,
And notice how *slapper* is modern for *slag*,
What was once *groovy* has now become *cool*,
A *todger* is favoured to *willy* or *tool*,
How *good* became *bad* was a strange circumstance,
And what was once *naff* is, in modern terms, *pants*,
It's great to be *wicked* the way the young talk,
You're never a *wally*, but always a *dork*,
A *chick* is a *babe*, and *Joe Cool* is a *dude*,
The youngsters all *honk*, while the rest of us *spewed*,
We used to *wind down*, now we choose to *chill out*,
A *dog* of today is an ugly, old *trout*,
A *slash* is a *whizz*, while a *dump* was a *crap*,
A *fanny*'s a *beaver*, a *wank*'s now a *slap*,
But none of these things will affect me, of course,
I won't talk in slang, by volition or force,
I find it amazing how words change so fast,
I would have gone on, but I couldn't be *arsed*.

Graham Eastaugh 19/6/99

# Nothing much doing

"How long will it take you repairing my van?"
"How long is a piece of string?" answered the man,
I then enquired as to the price of the job,
He said I should talk to a person called Bob,
I asked him where Bob was. He said: "I don't know,
The last time I saw him was hours ago,"
By now I was angry, and losing my head,
"I hear what you're saying," he sluggishly said,
I earnestly told him I'd tried to be nice,
It's just that I had to be quoted a price,
"I see where you're coming from, really I do,"
The man then replied, as he stopped for a brew,
My blood pressure soared; he was driving me mad,
His attitude seemed to me hopelessly bad,
He finished his cuppa, and then with a smile,
He told me I'd have to bear with him a while,
He mentioned the parts, and the time it would take,
And outlined the VAT charges to make,
He looked at the clock, and then filled me with sorrow,
And said with a smirk: "Can you come back tomorrow?"
The way that the bulk of our country is run,
I can't believe anything ever gets done,
It's possible mine's a too critical call,
But most people seem to be doing sod all.

Graham Eastaugh 15/6/01

# Rough justice

The newt went ballistic; the parrot was mad,
The rat almost anything other than glad,
The reason they kicked up a terrible stink,
Was being accused of enjoying a drink,
They'd heard about humans as pissed as a rat,
A newt or a parrot, but never a cat,
Why such a comparison baffled them much,
For alcohol's something that none of them touch,
The parrot protested aloud: "Don't you see?
When humans get arseholed, they're likened to *me,*
I want all this slanderous nonsense to stop,
'Cause even at Christmas, I don't touch a drop."
The newt, his head nodding, had clearly agreed,
He couldn't quite see this comparative need,
The rat lost his temper, and started to cuss:
"I can't understand why they think they're like us,
We're strictly teetotal, while *they* drink like fish,
So being compared to their kind I don't wish."
A fish shouted: "Hang on, we don't drink at all!"
The judge then for silence decided to call,
He'd had a right skinful, and felt really pissed,
He found it ironic his state had been missed,
He called an adjournment; then threw out the case,
Then travelled home soberly out of his face.

Graham Eastaugh 8/6/01

# Too much too young

The kids of today don't live life as we did,
Life's totally changed since when I was a kid,
They grow up so fast, and they're free to run wild,
They seem to have so little time as a child,
When I was their age I was playing with toys,
And hanging around with a few other boys,
Annoying the neighbours, and climbing up trees,
We really had fun; we could do as we'd please,
We'd have a good kick-about over the park,
And always be tucked up in bed before dark,
We had little money, but that mattered not,
As long as these brilliant childhoods we'd got,
But look at things now; they're behaving like mugs,
They're drinking and shagging and doing hard drugs,
They think they're so smart, but they don't have a clue,
It's sad they miss out on the things that I'd do,
They've plenty of money, but where's all the fun?
Their childhoods are over before they've begun,
I truly feel sorry for kids of today,
They don't get the chance to enjoy life my way,
But that's how it is - they're the losers, not me,
They've missed out on having a childhood, you see,
I'm so sympathetic, but what hurts me most:
Mine wasn't a similar childhood to boast.

Graham Eastaugh 6/11/01

# A womb with a view

Listen to me, I've a story to tell,
My tale, to a lot of you, might ring a bell,
You see I'm a uterus, causing me gloom,
I'll tell you just why I'm an unhappy womb,
There once was a time I'd a smile on my face,
I felt quite at ease, and had plenty of space,
But out of the blue came a frightening deed,
A purple intruder implanted a seed,
I felt all confused 'cause it wasn't my fault,
My once-a-month cycle had come to a halt,
I hadn't stopped pedalling - what can I say?
I did nothing wrong; it just happened that way,
An embryo formed, and my space became cramped,
My unwelcome guest was now firmly encamped,
My awful position was still unresolved,
And then, without warning, a foetus evolved,
Then, after a while, I brought action about,
I tightened my muscles, and squeezed the thing out,
Although I was empty, my anger had soared,
'Cause somehow I'd grown an umbilical cord!
I then noticed something to add to my stress:
A hideous gynaecological mess!
I'm not too aggrieved, though I felt it unfair,
I just wish my owner had taken more care.

Graham Eastaugh 26/1/00

# Kids' stuff

I sat all alone, looking back on the past,
And thought that it's frightening how time goes so fast,
I called on my mind to enlighten me so,
Of things that took place such a long time ago,
I'd play knockdown ginger, and act such a fool,
And try to pee highest against a brick wall,
I'd get up to all sorts of mischief at nights,
And I and my pals would have 'doggy do' fights,
We'd meet in the street, and swap bubble gum stickers,
We'd lie on the pavement, and peek at girls' knickers,
We'd trample through puddles; we never seemed dry,
And pulled the girls' ponytails, making them cry,
We'd play off ground touch, and we'd say 'pretty please',
And all of our trousers had holes in their knees,
We'd all gather round an old H&E mag,
And take it in turns for a puff on a fag,
We'd often go scrumping, like real Mr Bigs,
And make some hoax phone calls to piss off the pigs,
We'd pester the locals for car cleaning jobs,
And sometimes we'd show one another our knobs,
I think of those times with my head in a haze,
I'd love to return to those halcyon days,
Whatever goes on in my lifetime from here,
I'll always remember that summer last year.

Graham Eastaugh 11/10/99

# Simple minds

We all know the shape of our planet today,
But this train of thought wasn't always the way,
For not long ago, in historical terms,
They thought it was flat, as our hindsight affirms,
We find it so funny they saw things as so,
They must have been stupid in failing to know,
But how would *we* know if we hadn't been told?
The following thoughts then began to unfold:
Without television, or photos from space,
Or *any* pictorial proof put in place,
Just how would we know we're on spherical ground?
And who in their right mind would think the world's round?
The oceans don't spill, so a logical mind,
Would scarcely conclude we're of globular kind,
Our knowledge was once next to nothing at all,
So who'd understand gravitational pull?
Wherever we travel, it seems every time,
Our route never takes on a circular line,
So why would a person from eras long gone,
Think anything other than flat Earth we're on?
Of all the vast knowledge we proudly possess,
We've simply been programmed that way, more or less,
We know what we're told; it's as simple as that,
So why's it so funny *they* thought Earth was flat?

Graham Eastaugh 12/3/00

# After the love has gone

"Still," I explained, his expression so pained,
"There's plenty more fish in the sea,
I'm sure, given time, things will pan out just fine,
And not feeling down on your luck is the key."
"But I love her," he said, "and want none in her stead,
And refuse to believe that we're finished,
I made her my wife for the rest of my life,
Now I'm told that our partnership's swiftly diminished."
I urged him to have a few beers down the pub,
And then offered some words of advice:
"Get a grip of yourself; it's not good for the health,
To be needlessly putting your love life on ice,
You can't let a bird mess your head up like this,
I don't want to hear any bull,
Just dust yourself down, and then go into town,
And get yourself, quick as you can, on the pull."
I started to think I was wasting my breath,
His response was a tad out of hand,
He openly cried as he brushed me aside,
And then bluntly implied I did not understand,
I told him to buck up, whilst warning him thus:
"You'll drag us all down at this rate,
I hope you're not gonna be this bloody glum,
On the day of the funeral, mate."

Graham Eastaugh 10/1/08

# Capital growth

What killed the dinosaurs? No one's quite sure,
Perhaps a huge asteroid gave them what for?
Or maybe a virus deprived them of breath?
Or was it an ice age that froze them to death?
Whatever it was, and whatever it's not,
I've lately been racking my brains quite a lot,
And after a few months of utter confusion,
I finally came to a startling conclusion,
I've recently studied some history tapes,
Of human development since we were apes,
How each generation has increased in height,
I suddenly thought of the dinosaurs' plight,
Our fathers were generally shorter than us,
And so it goes on through the centuries, thus,
In my estimation, there'll soon come a day,
When human existence has all passed away,
We can't last forever increasing in size,
Something must change, or we'll meet our demise,
And that's when I thought of a long time ago,
Like six-and-a-half million decades or so,
The dinosaurs didn't get wiped out at all,
It's just through the years they got too bloody tall,
Their hearts couldn't take their expansion outside,
It came to the point when they dropped down and died,
We humans are taking a similar course,
The dinosaurs might have been our size at source,
And if this is so, there's no simple solution,
Our destiny lies with our own evolution,
But all this conjecture's a long time from now,
We'll all be long gone from this life anyhow,
The end of the human race won't be *our* loss,
So what killed the dinosaurs? Who gives a toss!

Graham Eastaugh 15/6/99

# A matter of time

We're frequently told to take care of our health,
The message is simple: look after yourself,
That drinking and smoking take years off our lives,
Without certain things how longevity thrives,
We're urged to live sensibly; exercise more,
Avoid fatty foods is the unwritten law,
In healthier lifestyles we all should engage,
And that way we'll live to a much older age,
Then one day when eighty or ninety or so,
We'll get to live life we'd not otherwise know,
We'll reap all the fruits of our sensible days,
And revel in octogenarian ways,
We'll live in a home at extortionate cost,
A midsummer morning will feel like a frost,
Our bladders we might not be able to hold,
Our only companions unbearably old,
We'll relish the fact we've been put out to grass,
Whenever a carer is wiping our arse,
We might be subjected to losing our mind,
Familiar faces are long left behind,
For that's how it is when we're over the hill,
We've nothing to offer except time to kill,
These may be uncomfortable thoughts to profess,
But that's what old age will become more or less,
To me loss of dignity's desperately sad,
So maybe a premature end's not so bad?
We'd each of us hate to lose all self-respect,
But if we stay healthy that's what to expect,
For good health can only go on for so long,
You can't spend an entire lifetime on song,
So anyone bringing old age into play,
Is bound to be somebody's burden one day,

To be old and unloved is everyone's fear,
But that's where we're heading with each passing year,
And if that's a prospect to worry about,
Then surely it's best to enjoy - then get out?
However we live life we'll still end up dead,
And surely the picture I've drawn is to dread?
So given the fact that there's nothing to lose,
My thinking is stick with the fags and the booze.

Graham Eastaugh 2/12/01

# Itchy and scratchy

When I was a boy in my formative days,
I wanted my body to change in some ways,
Although my head had hair aplenty on show,
I wanted some curly and short ones below,
I'd noticed a few of the lads in my year,
Had deepening voices while hair would appear,
In places where I still had no hair at all,
And girls seemed to view them as hunks of the school,
I started to feel like a dog with no bone,
I desperately wanted some hairs of my own,
I wanted to learn what my right arm was for,
The nickname of 'Baldy' I wanted no more,
But now as I live as a middle-aged man,
I'm not sure my pubic desires went to plan,
Although I was keen on the plus points it's true,
I wasn't aware there'd be minuses too,
The chaos they caused with my hormones was mad,
I'd suddenly sprouted a spare Brillo pad,
I now have to zip up my flies with such care,
And crabs have been known to take holidays there,
They started out fluffy and cute in a way,
But why did they have to turn wiry and grey?
They seem good for nothing but causing me grief,
And how do they sometimes get stuck in my teeth?
So now I've decided to shave to the skin,
From now on my days as a 'smoothie' begin,
The fact is when shove tends to supersede push,
A bird in the hand is worth two in the bush.

Graham Eastaugh 5/4/03

# Funny old name

The man in the pub told his mate at the bar,
He'd recently purchased a second-hand car,
From a bloke known as Chalkie on Saturday night,
And said that the car seller's surname was White,
He told him that Chalkie was good friends with Smudge,
Whose surname was Smith like his father, a judge,
Who part-owned with Dusty a holiday villa,
And said that the surname of Dusty was Miller,
He told him that Dusty lived next door to Bill,
Whose surname was Bailey, whose real name was Phil,
He told him the car hadn't cost him too much,
As Chalkie was selling it cheaply for Dutch,
He told him that Dutch was a person called Jack,
Whose surname was Holland, who lived in a shack,
Who needed the money to pay off a fine,
For starting a fight when he'd drunk too much wine,
He told him that Dutch had been nicked by a bobby,
Whose friends in the Force all referred to as Nobby,
He said he felt sorry that Dutch had been caught,
But that's how his second-hand car had been bought,
He said that the constable's nickname was so,
His friend interjected: "Don't tell me - I know,
His surname was Clark?" And then much to his shock,
His friend said the reason's a thirteen-inch cock.

Graham Eastaugh 17/12/01

# Fashion

The subject of fashion's a curious thing,
It's strange what response an appearance can bring,
How one thing's deemed cool, while another one's not,
How something looks naff, while another looks hot,
It's hard to explain, but it's just how it goes,
That everyone's judged by the choice of their clothes,
It's not just our clothing that gets us uptight,
The timing of wearing them has to be right,
I'm due for a trip to a club very soon,
I hardly go out, so I'm over the moon,
It's years since I last ventured out and about,
I fear I've lost track of what's 'in' and what's 'out',
Should trousers be baggy or straight at the bottom?
Are ties thin or wide? I've simply forgotten,
And jacket lapels should be broad, or be slim?
Should colours be bright? Or should colours be dim?
And what of the height of the heels on my shoes?
Are waistcoats the trend, or not currently used?
And just to prevent me committing a sin,
Are shirts hanging out? Or are shirt-tails tucked in?
I find it amusing the fashions we keep,
We're socially pressured to follow like sheep,
'Cause if we decide not to copy the rule,
We open ourselves up to mass ridicule,
What's now out of fashion was once all the rage,
What's trendy tomorrow's a history page,
Is everyone stupid? I'm not really sure,
Whatever's called 'new', someone's worn it before,
I've found a good way of avoiding the trap,
How no one can tell me my dress sense is crap,
I'm giving my whole public look a revamp,
By joining the ranks of a naturist camp.

Graham Eastaugh 28/4/99

# Verbal abuse

It's funny the way that a human mind works,
How each individual has varying quirks,
But one thing we all share, with cunning disguise,
Is spending our lives telling little white lies,
No one's excluded; we're all just the same,
Diplomacy's always the name of the game,
Our brains tell us one thing, but stay well aloof,
And direct our mouths into dodging the truth,
We all tell our loved ones they're right when they're wrong,
And tell them they're great when they're clearly off song,
We say that we're happy, when really we're sad,
And say we feel good, when we really feel bad,
And think of the times we appreciate wit,
When really we're thinking: "You boring old git!"
And who has the guts to destroy a girl's heart,
And tell her her dress makes her look like a tart?
We talk to our bosses with utmost respect,
While praying our hatred is hard to detect,
We smile at our neighbours, and ask if they're well,
But inwardly wish them a journey to hell,
We'd love to be honest, but know that we can't,
The truth really hurts, so we choose to enchant,
Our mouths always seem to betray our desires,
The bottom line is: we're all born bloody liars.

Graham Eastaugh 2/10/99

# Courting disaster

A long time ago, in my last days at school,
Like most adolescents, I wanted it all,
I'd done all my schooling; now life had begun,
The dark days were over; I wanted some fun,
I had little money, but hormones galore,
I knew lots of girls, but required a bit more,
My feelings were what every youngster expects,
I wanted a friend of the opposite sex,
I looked everywhere, and attended all places,
I studied all forms, and examined all faces,
But hard as I tried, I appeared to be stuck,
I had to face facts; I was right out of luck,
A friend of mine told me he'd like to assist,
And wrote down the names of some girls in a list,
He told me that each was a very good friend,
I went about bringing my quest to an end,
Runaround Sue was a little too frisky,
While Moonshine Sally drank far too much whisky,
And one of the gang seemed a bit too divine,
So I didn't waste time chasing Sweet Caroline,
And Dirty Diana was much too obscene,
I didn't know where Poison Ivy had been,
I found Lady Lynda too posh in the main,
And thought of the law when I saw Baby Jane,
Amazing Grace then put my head in a whirl,
I'd never met such an adorable girl,
Then one of her friends gave my hopes a huge dent,
And said what 'Amazing' in Grace really meant,
My confidence sank; I was losing my touch,
And even Dear Prudence was charging too much,
I felt really down, with my head at a loss,
And Black Pudding Bertha was not worth a toss,
I went home that night in a sad state of mind,
A suitable lady I just couldn't find,
I couldn't believe I'd done anything wrong,
Just didn't seem able to sing the right song.

Graham Eastaugh 18/1/00

# Born lucky

I've always been baffled by public acclaim,
For talented people with fortune and fame,
How most of us worship incredible skill,
And marvel at folk who aren't run-of-the-mill,
The way that I see things, we've got it all wrong,
Our praise has been somewhat misplaced all along,
I don't wish to take away anyone's glory,
I'd just like to offer my view of the story,
If someone's not born with a good singing voice,
They'll never sing well; they just won't have a choice,
Though practice makes perfect, it won't mean a thing,
If someone's tone-deaf, and unable to sing,
The same rule applies to all sportsmen of note,
Without innate talent, they've no cause to gloat,
With every ability, rules are alike,
You can't cycle fast if you don't have a bike,
Mozart made music that gives us a lift,
But was he so grand, or just blessed with a gift?
Ali was awesome; the finest to date,
The planet was spellbound, but was he *born* great?
I know that the famous work hard at their arts,
But where would they be without privileged starts?
We'd all love success, but we don't have the means,
You have to inherit the relevant genes,
So why do we idolise people with class?
In my way of thinking, the logic's a farce,
And why should it be that they're lauded like gods,
When, really, they're just bloody fortunate sods?

Graham Eastaugh 16/9/99

# Man on the moon

There's many a person who thinks that one day,
To cope with increased population we may,
Alleviate Earth's overcrowding quite soon,
By sending off some of our race to the moon,
We'll introduce colonies living in space,
Have lunar communities firmly in place,
We've all sorts of wild innovations in store,
And, happily, Earth will be crowded no more,
There's one tiny problem that troubles me so,
It won't be much fun for the first ones to go,
It might be exciting, but that won't atone,
For spending the rest of their lives all alone,
And that's when the following thought came to mind:
If I had my way, I'd be hugely inclined,
To using the moon as we once treated Oz,
The moon could become how Australia was,
We'd pack off our criminals; not to return,
A perfect solution, albeit quite stern,
There's bound to be many who think it too grave,
But what an incentive to learn to behave?
And then in a couple of centuries-plus,
A new land will grow, and develop like us,
To England their people will buy an air ticket,
And give us a bloody good thrashing at cricket.

Graham Eastaugh 23/3/00

# It's a wonderful life?

Of all human beings existing today,
I wonder how many can honestly say,
They live as they please, without any restraint,
And life is a beautiful picture to paint?
For most of us do things we don't want to do,
With 'freedom' confined to a very small few,
We all require money, and therefore we work,
But money discounted, we'd most of us shirk,
Employment can swallow up much of our lives,
It's often the case animosity thrives,
For how many people with hand on their heart,
Can say that their colleagues and friends aren't apart?
And how many people can truthfully voice,
Their social companions are always by choice?
And how many live life concealing a frown,
With family links often tying them down?
The way we exist can be hard to believe,
For how many live with their heart on their sleeve?
I'm sure it's a fact that we're mostly the same,
That all of our lives, we're just pawns in a game,
Of course, I'm not saying it's all doom and gloom,
There's many a high to the grave from the womb,
For most of us savour our days at their prime,
But sometimes it seems we're just wasting our time.

Graham Eastaugh 29/2/00

# Words of wisdom

I remember the day when they first heard the news,
They thought it the most disrespectful of views,
The theory that made all the shit hit the fan,
Was anthropoid apes are related to Man,
They felt so aggrieved that in all bar the name,
The two groups are almost exactly the same,
Though DNA proved it, they made such a fuss,
They couldn't believe they'd been likened to *us,*
The apes went bananas; the monkeys went nuts,
The chimps and baboons were exposing their butts,
The gibbons went apeshit; orangutans wild,
I've never seen so many primates so riled,
A massive gorilla was beating his chest,
And all of the lemurs were none too impressed,
They all felt insulted to different degrees,
The aye-ayes were so mad they swung from the trees,
A gibbon protested to apelike applause:
"Though no intellectuals, we never start wars,
We only place value on things that we need,
We never succumb to material greed,
We've no inhibitions; we act as we feel,
We don't have a calorie-count every meal,
We're not image-conscious; we're not stressed a jot,
So what an affront to be grouped with you lot."
The humans were stunned, but it forced them to think,
Their hairy opponent had caused such a stink,
We think we're advanced in whatever we do,
But, sadly, the words of the gibbon were true.

Graham Eastaugh 28/3/01

# Making waves

I'm fed up of hearing how smart dolphins are,
Intelligence-wise how they're way above par,
'Cause, firstly, I'd like to ask how do we know?
And, secondly, where's the proof telling us so?
They live underwater, and don't come on land,
Their cousins, the whales, get marooned on the sand,
They swim everywhere, every move that they make,
They've no public transport at all, for Christ's sake!
They don't live in houses; they can't even speak,
They don't even care where they go for a leak,
And though coarse remarks I do *not* wish to pass,
How many dolphins can wipe their own arse?
They've no manual skills, and they can't read or write,
They've never experienced jet-propelled flight,
They haven't worked out how to cook their meals yet,
They can't use a tin-opener either I bet,
They're easily captured; we take them as slaves,
We're clearly the ones who are ruling the waves,
They do what we say; they've no minds of their own,
So, surely, this theory they're bright's overblown?
I'll never subscribe to this notion - not me,
I've just proved it nonsense I'm sure you'll agree,
The truth is their species is normal at best,
That's good for sod all, just the same as the rest.

Graham Eastaugh 9/11/01

# Always look on the bright side of life

A number of people who know me quite well,
May secretly feel that my life must be hell,
You see, I've been struck by a nervous disease,
Now nothing I do any more is with ease,
Though not paralysed, my appearance conceals,
The fact I depend on a chair sporting wheels,
True, you could say that I haven't been blessed,
With some of the fortune of most of the rest,
I'd never pretend I've the life of my dreams,
But maybe my fate's not as bad as it seems,
Everyone's sure that my world's short of glory,
But let me put forward my side of the story:
As every year passes, my chances get thinner,
Of bursting the net with a Cup Final winner,
Or winning the Open on ten under par,
Or reaching the status of rock superstar,
But all is not lost, I've some great days ahead,
I'm hardly confined to a lifetime in bed,
I haven't the health I'd assumed as a boy,
But think about some of the perks I enjoy,
Working for money I've managed to scrub,
I've always a seat when I go to a pub,
The hour I get up is now something I choose,
I never get shit on the soles of my shoes,
Lunchtime TV I can lap up at last,
And standing in queues is a thing of the past,
Each public appearance makes strangers agog,
And sometimes I get my own personal bog,
It's easy to take all the weight off my feet,
And little old ladies are ever so sweet,
I don't move a muscle, but don't think I'm sour,

I manage to travel at four miles per hour,
So save all your tears; I've a wonderful life,
My days are bereft of all trouble and strife,
Think of the future and quit reminiscing,
And think of the things that you poor sods are missing.

Graham Eastaugh 27/2/99

# Open to interpretation

"We're packed in like humans," said Stan the sardine,
A Liverpool fan said: "I know what you mean,"
"I'm sick as a parrot," said Porky the pig,
The date shouted loudly: "I don't give a fig,"
The dragon complained he was bored with his life,
The man said his missus was giving him strife,
He called her a dragon; the dragon said: "What?
She might be a cow, but a dragon she's *not,*"
The wife of the man said: "Don't call me a witch,"
A dog interrupted and called her a bitch,
The woman took umbrage and called him a hound,
A son of a bitch started sniffing around,
He said it was likely she's more of a sow,
"You're all talking bull," said the spouse of the cow,
"My head's really sore," said the big grizzly bear,
The stallion seemed to be having a mare,
The rabbits announced they were breeding like rats,
The vampire accused them of driving him bats,
He said that the woman was more like a dog,
"I'd say she was more of a trout," said the hog,
The woman, dejected, was walking away,
The dog said the words every bird has its day,
The sardine suggested some kippers for tea,
The trout said: "It sounds a bit fishy to me."

Graham Eastaugh 6/7/01

# Leading by example

We all tell our children they're not to tell lies,
It's solid advice, and of little surprise,
As dutiful adults, it's our job to teach,
But very few practise the things that we preach,
The moment we've taught them the value of truth,
We tell them some fat bloke will land on the roof,
And come down the chimney on each Christmas Eve,
We go to all lengths to make sure they believe,
We even fill stockings, and do all we can,
To help make look real this imaginary man,
We say this intruder is no one to fear,
But warn them of strangers the rest of the year,
And when a young child has a tooth that comes out,
We say that there might be a fairy about,
Delivering cash when the child is in bed,
In place of the tooth, underneath the child's head,
We spin silly stories of heaven and hell,
We do the same things about Jesus as well,
We say there's a god, but there really can't be,
If all the news items are true on TV,
But children aren't fools; they catch on in the end,
And work out the stories were only pretend,
Above all, they learn in the future they must,
Treat all that they hear with enormous distrust,
So why should we wonder when kids are so bold,
In never believing a thing they are told?
We're solely to blame, and the kids not one bit,
They started their lives with their heads full of shit.

Graham Eastaugh 3/4/99

# Insult to injury

"Does he take sugar?" said the girl by the till,
To the young lady with me...if looks could kill!
"He can speak for himself," she angrily snapped,
The girl by the till's knuckles suitably rapped,
I sat in my wheelchair; my face slightly red,
Embarrassed the girl hadn't asked me instead,
I wasn't impressed, although not at all sore,
I'd witnessed this kind of behaviour before,
I couldn't believe the insensitive way,
The girl by the till chose the words that she'd say,
It's not that the girl by the till was disgraced,
It's just that her words were severely misplaced,
I answered: "No thanks," as I don't like a scene,
She meant no offence, so I shouldn't be mean,
I gave some advice as she served me my drink,
And told her in future to just stop and think,
She said she was sorry she'd caused me such pain,
And told me she wouldn't insult me again,
It's not that her question got under my skin,
But why would she think I'd take sugar with gin?

Graham Eastaugh 27/12/01

118

# Mustn't grumble

I was sitting at home, feeling down on my luck,
And thought to myself I was stuck in a rut,
Life was quite boring; my days were the same,
My very existence was painfully tame,
But all of a sudden, my mood turned to glee,
There had to be others much worse off than me,
I shouldn't delight at another's expense,
But hear out my story; you'll see it makes sense,
I thought of the tapeworm; the life that it had,
And quickly concluded mine wasn't so bad,
My days might be dull, and quite uninteresting,
At least I'm not living in someone's intestine,
My mind took me back to a long time ago,
I had a pet cat with a bell and a bow,
Everyone loved him, but then he'd turn sinner,
And lift up his tail during family dinner,
Whenever this happened, it made us all squirm,
For just by the arsehole: a wriggling worm,
Of course, at the time, I just thought of myself,
I thought the worm must be enjoying itself,
But now I look back, that just wasn't the case,
In front of his mates, the worm must have lost face,
Then after a while, he would dry up and die,
Then drop to the floor, where for weeks he would lie,
A dignified ending was out of the question,
And everyone chuckled at such a suggestion,
Instead of a coffin, his final manoeuvre,
Was being sucked up by a pipe on the Hoover,
The life of a tapeworm's a sobering thought,
They don't watch the telly, or play any sport,
Which just goes to show the old adage is true,
There's always somebody much worse off than you.

Graham Eastaugh 8/3/99

119

# The rest is history

Always beware a religious fanatic,
Of bigots whose thinking is rigidly static,
Of people who practise their faith with such zest,
Of zealots who think their religion's the best,
Of people whose bigotry's built to bequeath,
Of people whose hatred is worn on their sleeve,
Of people who simply refuse to be moved,
To questioning something that hasn't been proved,
Of people who don't have a mind of their own,
Of people with hearts manufactured of stone,
Of people who revel in conflict and war,
Of people who fear what democracy's for,
For history tells us it's always the same,
Whatever the conflict, religion's to blame,
Belief in a faith that's essentially blind,
A cover for people with evil in mind,
I'm not into dreaming; I know things won't change,
I just find it all so depressingly strange,
The lessons we learn are forgotten so fast,
And all that's ahead is what's already passed.

Graham Eastaugh 30/10/01

# Intimate strangers

We met at a lonely hearts club one weekend,
I wanted an unattached girl to befriend,
I bought her a drink; then I asked her her name,
It turned out our interests were roughly the same,
She liked eating out, with the odd glass of wine,
Her love of Max Bygraves was equal to mine,
She liked doing crosswords and needlework, too,
The way we were matched seemed too good to be true,
And then when the end of the evening arose,
I offered to escort her home, as it goes,
I made the suggestion we meet the next week,
And planted a 'cheerio' kiss on her cheek,
She told me she couldn't stand being alone,
And took to inviting me into her home,
She opened the door and I followed her in,
And that's when the following tale would begin:
She tickled my tackle; then unzipped my passion,
And five minutes later we did doggy-fashion,
Her carnal fulfilment was fully assured,
Not one of her cavities went unexplored,
We'd only just met but I knew it was love,
Our parts seemed to fit like a hand in a glove,
She went like a train as I bucked like a bull,
My baggage compartment was no longer full,
I didn't stop thrusting; she didn't stop screaming,
The chandeliers shook and the windows were steaming,
Our animal instincts were freely let loose,
As I was all tadpoles and she was all juice,
We panted and puffed as we rolled on the floor,
The skin on our genitals soon was red raw,
We'd so much electrical friction about,
That even our down-below hair straightened out,

We finally ended our love-making session,
And that's when she made an appalling confession,
She knew her admission would drive us apart,
And what she would tell me would shatter my heart,
I thought she'd been honest but this wasn't so,
I said it was best I get dressed and then go,
I'd truly believed her but now felt a fool,
She wasn't a fan of Max Bygraves at all.

Graham Eastaugh 21/3/02

# Down in the mouth

"Try to relax," said the man with a grin,
Then he started this bloody great drill,
I said to the dentist: "Before you begin,
Allow me to jump from this sill."
I leapt out the window, and made my escape,
The dentist said: "Don't be afraid,"
I held up my fingers to make a V shape,
And thought what a good choice I'd made,
But why should a dentist instil so much fear,
When clearly there's nothing to dread?
Our lives are at risk every day of the year,
But somehow our fears are all shed,
Each trip in a car could bring possible doom,
But how many tremble inside?
For negative thoughts we would never give room,
But freeze when we hear 'open wide',
I don't have the answer; I wish that I did,
So on this debate I'll stay quiet,
All trips to the dentist in future I'll rid,
And stick to my soup-only diet.

Graham Eastaugh 10/1/00

# Fame

Slowly but surely, though quite immaturely,
The bulldog clip clamped on his penis securely,
He desperately wanted his moment of fame,
And thought this his last chance of making his name,
The record he sought stood at forty-nine hours,
Belonging to someone called Dick 'Nobby' Powers,
Should Nobby's incredible feat be surpassed,
Then Willie O'Toole would be famous at last,
He'd failed an audition for Britain's Got Talent,
And tried to get rich on that show with Chris Tarrant,
He'd tried The X Factor, and Big Brother, too,
But failed to find fame in whatever he'd do,
He'd tried to bed Jordan but got the thumbs down,
And rued the fact Jade was no longer around,
As Fathers 4 Justice had no more stunts planned,
He'd claimed a few sightings of Madeleine McCann,
His record attempt was now well underway,
His knob being clamped for well over a day,
He looked quite composed, although no one knew how,
And casually wiped beads of sweat from his brow,
However, the pressure would finally tell,
It soon became clear he was feeling unwell,
He wobbled; he swayed, and fell flat on his back,
He threw in the towel as his todger turned black,
Obsession with fame is the norm of our time,
As if anonymity's almost a crime,
Celebrity status is so overblown,
There's no shame at all in not being well-known,
So what of the fate of young Willie O'Toole?
He ended up seeing a doctor, that's all,
He had to accept that he'd never be famous,
Just rather a desperately sad ignoramus.

Graham Eastaugh 2/10/09

# Behind the mask

Generally speaking, more often than not,
We humans are mostly a civilised lot,
We live side by side, coexisting quite well,
But what lies ahead of us, no one can tell,
A long time ago, at the dawn of our race,
We got by with minimal goodwill and grace,
The essence of life was survival alone,
And enemies simply were persons unknown,
But since our beginning, we've mellowed so much,
With those days of savagery way out of touch,
We've mastered compassion, and learnt to be kind,
And left all our animal instincts behind,
But were things to change, and calamity call,
We found ourselves forced with our backs to the wall,
I wonder how long it would all take before,
Our animal instincts would come to the fore?
When push comes to shove, we'd do all to survive,
Our natural instinct is staying alive,
So given an instance of serious threat,
The welfare of others we'd quickly forget,
We're hostile by nature, as history implies,
Our outward appearance is just a disguise,
We've slowly conditioned ourselves to abide,
It's frightening to think what we harbour inside,
We've only to glance a few years in the past,
To conjure up visions to leave us aghast,
Like Bosnia, Kosovo, East Timor too,
To show us the evil we humans can do,
Whoever you are, evil's always so near,
It just needs the right circumstance to appear,
Life is survival; we play for high stakes,
We'll always resort to whatever it takes,
Of all the most hideous acts you have heard,
Of human atrocities crudely occurred,
That given an instance of push comes to shove,
I wonder how many *you're* capable of?

Graham Eastaugh 13/3/00

# Suffer the little children

When I worked for a living a few years ago,
I felt at a huge disadvantage, you know,
'Cause being a man, I was dealt a weak hand,
And didn't have options as others had planned,
So hear out my story; I'll try to explain,
Exactly the reason I used to complain,
It's not my desire to be pouring out scorn,
I just feel aggrieved by the way I was born,
I worked in an office with females and males,
But felt an enormous imbalance of scales,
For while we were treated the same in our pay,
The girls would have one vital trump card to play,
My job was all right, but I wanted to shirk,
My biggest ambition was packing up work,
But what could I do? I had nowhere to run,
I had to earn cash, so my options were none,
The girls, on the other hand, weren't stuck like me,
They held certain cards to get out of jail free,
For pregnancy offered a means of escape,
A journey that none of us fellas could take,
But maybe quite soon we'll be in the same boat,
A news item made me sit up and take note,
It said that a medical breakthrough was here,
How child-bearing times for a man were now near,
They say that a foetus could grow in the bowel,
A wonder of science, if a little bit foul,
And, after a while, when it runs out of room,
The baby will then be transferred to a womb,
It's too late for me; I don't work any more,
It's still nice to know that they've levelled the score,
That men are no longer bogged down in the mire,
We've suddenly got a new way to retire,
But hang on a moment. How selfish is that?
I'm starting to sound like a self-centred prat,

I hadn't considered the baby itself,
Its feelings, its pride and, above all, its health,
Now, many a person's existence is crap,
With so many caught in the poverty trap,
There's many a life that's enjoyed not one bit,
But surely it's wrong to start off in the shit?

Graham Eastaugh 24/10/99

# A time and a place

Attitudes change with the passing of time,
What once was acceptable, now is a crime,
A look back through history illustrates this,
How hideous acts once weren't seen as amiss,
Two thousand years past, with most evil designs,
Christians by Romans were thrown to the lions,
Judging with hindsight, those times are abhorred,
But living in Rome, it was all above board,
The same thing applies to the Christian Crusades,
For, then, they were viewed as the most just of raids,
The same can be said of the British Empire,
When, not long ago, we claimed all we'd desire,
And what about slavery? What a disgrace!
A fair way to treat an inferior race,
But speaking in retrospect, utter disgust,
Historically speaking, it's unsettled dust,
I wonder how one day *our* lives will be seen?
A civilised race? Or behaviour obscene?
We think we're exemplars of goodwill to all,
But do we believe it? Or just try to fool?
Will folk of the future, and faraway times,
Describe with revulsion our animal crimes?
And how we treat plant life and insects to boot?
And will we be censured for slicing up fruit?

Graham Eastaugh 16/10/99

# The magic of modern medicine

I once had a friend with impeccable grammar,
Who, sadly for him, had a terrible stammer,
Whenever he spoke, certain words were delayed,
Which sometimes inspired cruel remarks to be made,
But then he decided to bring about change,
A trip to the doctor he chose to arrange,
He talked to an expert in problems with speech,
And hoped that an end to his stammer he'd reach,
But after a while, it had soon become clear,
An end to his plight wasn't anywhere near,
His therapy failed, though he'd tried all he could,
He had to face facts; it had done him no good,
Then just when he felt at the end of his rope,
Alternative medicine offered him hope,
He'd heard of a colleague who'd had some success,
By using these methods to cure him of stress,
My friend then decided to follow his lead,
And tried different methods to answer his need,
He tried homeopathy; herbalists too,
But got no result from whatever he'd do,
He tried acupuncture, but felt like a prick,
He drank his own urine, which made him feel sick,
He saw a psychiatrist; covered all ground,
But, just like the hypnotist, no cure was found,
Then just when it seemed that his last chance had gone,
A new kind of treatment he stumbled upon,
Its name I've forgotten, but he was quite sure,
That this time he'd found a miraculous cure,
A few Sundays later, we met as desired,
I bought him a drink, and politely enquired:
"How's the new treatment? Have you had any luck?"
And he answered: "Have I f...f...f...f...fuck!"

Graham Eastaugh 7/10/99

129

# An eye for an eye

With six billion people inhabiting Earth,
And death being vastly outnumbered by birth,
We must find a way of controlling our race,
By putting some positive action in place,
I haven't the answer; the question's too tough,
My mind isn't made of the right kind of stuff,
I nevertheless had a view of a sort,
And found myself faced with the following thought:
I know that this view will raise plenty of fears,
But why don't we turn back the clock a few years?
It's not a solution; that's something I lack,
But how about bringing the death sentence back?
We've numerous killers congesting our jails,
Who clearly will *never* get back on the rails,
They're sent there to satisfy public protection,
But why don't we give them a lethal injection?
It's not an ideal way to do things I know,
But why should a murderer trouble us so?
At least it's a way of avoiding more pain,
Ensuring all maniacs can't kill again,
I'm fully aware of objections from some,
Of wrongful convictions that can't be undone,
But rather than fear for an innocent's plight,
Just think of the pluses of those whose are right.

Graham Eastaugh 7/3/00

# A lesson in tact

I went to a function a few weeks ago,
With all sorts of high-profile people on show,
A fish out of water, I felt out of place,
When someone, quite rudely, invaded my space,
He barged his way through to the spot where I stood,
I looked for the door, but it did me no good,
He caught my attention, and then got my goat,
For some of his views really stuck in my throat,
He looked at the Chinese girl serving the drinks,
And told me he couldn't stand 'slanty-eyed Chinks,'
And, later that night, when the party's host spoke,
He laughed as he said she looked more like a bloke,
He put down the poor; his opinions were crude,
His actions displayed the most arrogant mood,
He ordered some food, and then sent it all back,
He'd heard that the person who'd cooked it was black,
I asked him if he had come here on his own,
He told me he strictly went nowhere alone,
He said that's the way he'd lived most of his life,
And then said he'd like me to meet with his wife,
He told me I knew her. I said: "I think not,"
He said that I'd probably seen her a lot,
I felt quite confused, and said: "What do you mean?"
And he said with utter disdain: "She's the Queen."

Graham Eastaugh 13/9/99

# The things we do for love

I've never been able to quite fathom out,
Why some of us seem to get carried away,
For one day per annum. I'm talking about,
The time of the year called St Valentine's Day,
But why should it be that for one day a year,
We need to be pressed into showing our love?
And is it romance, or just terrible fear,
That drives us to ensure we do just enough?
Now, men aren't immune, but the ladies are worse,
At treating this day with enormous respect,
For twenty-four hours, all our brain cells disperse,
And proving the power of love takes effect,
But woe betide any unfortunate man,
Who lets the day pass without doing his bit,
The love of his life will do all that she can,
To make sure the rest of his life becomes shit,
But why do we let ourselves follow like sheep?
Does anyone act off the cuff any more?
And isn't the ethic of forced passion cheap?
We're simply protecting our Brownie points score.

Graham Eastaugh 20/9/99

# Saint or sinner?

St George's day - what the hell's *that* all about?
I'm sure it's a day we can all do without,
It comes once a year, but it's hardly a perk,
As no one gets offered a day off from work,
It's all for a person who didn't exist,
Though many historians strongly insist,
There *was* such a man in 300 AD,
But, personally speaking, it's bollocks to me,
Whatever the answer, of one thing I'm sure,
One part of his story's too hard to ignore,
Whoever you are, and whatever your view,
You can't believe *all* of his tale to be true?
A fire-breathing dragon's to what I refer,
A fight to the death which was said to occur,
The dragon and George met on English terrain,
And George took a sword, and the dragon was slain,
But what a ridiculous story to tell,
A most unbelievable legend to sell,
But maybe our patron saint wasn't so bold,
And what really happened has never been told?
Instead of a dragon that threatened his life,
I wonder if maybe the 'beast' was his wife,
Who nagged him so much with inflammable breath,
That one day he 'lost it' and stabbed her to death?
Then, over the years, all the facts got distorted,
A dragon instead of his wife was reported,
His publicists felt he'd win much more respect,
Than for killing his missus for being henpecked,
Like so many things that took place in the past,
The margin for getting the facts wrong is vast,
I get no enjoyment from being so mean,
But how many dragons have *you* ever seen?

Graham Eastaugh 25/1/00

# Sunday, bloody Sunday

My time in this world has been quite a smooth ride,
A pleasant existence, it can't be denied,
But looking at life and its options today,
I'm starting to see things a different way,
I'm talking of one certain day of the week,
The day before Monday's about which I speak,
My mind took me back to my childhood afar,
Do kids of today know how lucky they are?
When I was a youngster we'd nothing to do,
Each Sunday was too bloody sad to be true,
It hardly seemed worthwhile our staying awake,
The only place open was church, for Christ's sake!
We couldn't eat takeaway food at our tables,
We'd shit on the telly like Anne of Green Gables,
We'd feel really bored; our existence forlorn,
We'd no such attraction as internet porn,
Our boredom was such it would cause us to weep,
We'd search for enjoyment by falling asleep,
All hope for excitement was pie in the sky,
A treat on a Sunday was watching paint dry,
The youngsters today think they've got it so tough,
Whatever the options, they're never enough,
But rather than moan about how things *might* be,
Just pause for a moment, and think about me.

Graham Eastaugh 17/3/01

# Out of proportion

Fanny Fantastic said: "Bob, you big spastic,
Do you fancy a pint after work?"
Bob said: "I do. I might even have two,
As overtime's something I'll happily shirk."
Dusty McCrusty, who'd always been fusty,
Said: "Fanny, I don't like your tone,
You called Bob a name, to your terrible shame,
Apologise now, and then leave him alone."
Fanny said: "What? What's the problem you've got?
The way I addressed him was fine,
He's big; his name's Bob; he's a spastic, you snob,
So each of my words was completely benign."
"I still think it's wrong," Miss McCrusty went on,
"It doesn't seem PC to me."
"But he's Bob, and he's big; he's a spastic, you prig,"
Fanny Fantastic declined to agree,
She went on: "You pests always think you know best,
You're always creating a scene,
You self-righteous gits really get on my tits,
Insisting we don't say the things that we mean."
Bob said: "She's right. I'm a spastic, alright,
And I'm Bob, and I'm on the large side,
So don't interfere, now I'm off for a beer,
With Fanny Fantastic, my soon-to-be bride."

Graham Eastaugh 7/11/01

# Pet puzzle

Life can be strange, full of puzzling things,
Like if they can't fly, why do penguins have wings?
And why is a nice person known as a brick?
And why do we drink, just to make ourselves sick?
Then, there is cricket. What's that all about?
You put a team in just to get them all out,
But this is the one that's as weird as it gets,
Why is it some of us humans keep pets?
Canines and cats, I can just understand,
But what about some of the rest?
All sorts of creatures inhabit the land,
But why share our dwellings at people's behest?
Hamsters and gerbils appear all the rage,
But what do they do except sit in a cage?
Rabbits and guinea pigs; they're just the same,
Doing sod all is their main claim to fame,
And what about birds, such as budgerigars?
They're no more exciting than insects in jars,
And why we keep fish is a mystery to me,
Unless they're for cooking with chips for our tea,
Pet owners talk of the comfort they bring,
How they're plenty of fun, though they don't do a thing,
They're some kind of company; it can't be denied,
But what sort of joy can a tortoise provide?
They live in the garden, their names on their shells,
And when they're on form, they're as boring as hell,
Why do we keep them? My mind's in a muddle,
They're ugly, they stink and they're crap for a cuddle,
So why is it animals live in our homes?
Why not be happy with stone garden gnomes?
Why have a pet? Someone answer me, please,
If I need companions, I'll stick to my fleas.

Graham Eastaugh 13/10/98

# Identity crisis

Sammy the snail wasn't feeling too well,
He suddenly noticed he hadn't a shell,
His awful predicament filled him with dread,
He urgently craved a roof over his head,
He met with some other snails; spoke of his plight,
And said he felt fine, but he didn't look right,
The others agreed, but they said not to fear,
They'd help in his search, till his shell would appear,
The snails held a meeting on where to look first,
They reached a decision, then duly dispersed,
They searched high and low, and left no stone unturned,
To find Sammy's shell they increasingly yearned,
But after a while, they were still out of luck,
They'd looked everywhere, and now seemed to be stuck,
The snails were confused, for they'd looked all around,
But, sadly, poor Sammy's shell couldn't be found,
Then one of the snails played a masterful card,
And pleaded for Sammy to think really hard,
And take his mind back on a trip through the past,
And try to recall where he saw his shell last,
Sammy replied in a way which would stun,
And told all the others he'd never had one,
The rest of the snails took exception to that,
And one of them said: "You're a slug, you daft prat!"

Graham Eastaugh 9/10/99

# Mitigating circumstances

I remember a long time ago as a child,
Enjoying attending such things as school fetes,
For one of the stalls let me act really wild,
By smashing up things such as saucers and plates,
Old crockery stalls are to what I refer,
Where missiles to hurl would be offered for sale,
Where frenzied behaviour would always occur,
And acts of destruction would always prevail,
It wasn't just kids, it was women and men,
And even old grannies would queue for a throw,
I'm certain it didn't occur to me then,
But now I'm much older, it came to me so:
We did as we did since the chance came about,
Our natural aggression could come to the fore,
With all inhibitions we acted without,
And no one need worry of breaking the law,
And thinking about it, I now understand,
How crass vandalism is easily bred,
On housing estates and suchlike in the land,
Where prospects are bleak, and there's boredom instead,
Wherever we're brought up, we tend to blend in,
It's lucky for many, but not so for some,
And how we turn out rests on where we begin,
Environments dictate the way we become.

Graham Eastaugh 4/2/00

# Size doesn't matter?

Mine's quite a bit bigger than others I know,
I wasn't concerned till a short time ago,
When all of a sudden to all other blokes,
My extra large one was the butt of their jokes,
A few years ago mine was envied by most,
Compared to the others I'd something to boast,
But then without warning, as if overnight,
The size of my thingummy *wasn't* all right,
Wherever I go people laugh in my face,
My thing being huge means there's no hiding place,
I guess that's how fickle we humans can be,
How quickly I fell from the top of the tree,
What used to be pride is embarrassment now,
Much more of this ridicule I won't allow,
I'll speak to a specialist dressed in disguise,
And sort out a deal for decreasing my size,
The last year or so has been absolute hell,
I literally never come out of my shell,
I'm fed up of something so massive to own,
And that's why I'm buying a new mobile phone.

Graham Eastaugh 26/12/01

# Eating disorder

The baby anteater said: "What's for tea, Mum?"
"Ants," said the mother. "I'll go and get some."
The baby said: "Surely not ants yet again?
It's ants every meal. I've got ants on the brain."
The mother said: "How can you be so ungrateful?
Just sit at the table. I'll get you a plateful,
I and your father work hard for your food,
And all you can do is be dreadfully rude."
"But Mum," said the baby, "It's not disrespect,
It's just not the balance of diet I expect,
I had ants for my breakfast, and ants for my brunch,
And, just for a change, I had ants for my lunch,
It's not just today, it was yesterday, too,
And the days before that. I'd like something new,
There's no way I want to upset you and Dad,
But ants are the only food I've ever had."
The mother then wore an expression of gloom,
And sent baby anteater up to his room,
His outburst was fierce. She was caught unawares,
She yelled at him as he ascended the stairs,
"How dare you behave like an ignorant lout,
What else can you eat with that bloody great snout?
The nerve of you kids is beyond my belief,
Remember - an anteater doesn't have teeth."
The baby said: "Sorry, Mum. Don't be upset,
I know what I am, but I sometimes forget,
I've learnt a harsh lesson, so don't look so grave,
I'll be a good boy, and I won't misbehave."
She gave him a cuddle, then *he* went to bed,
She kissed him good night, and he sheepishly said,
"I know my behaviour was awfully strange,
I just fancied something like chips for a change."

Graham Eastaugh 22/6/99

# Hope springs eternal

The lives of most people can feel quite a strain,
A humdrum existence for most in the main,
Of course, there's enjoyment and pleasure as well,
But tedious moments have more tales to tell,
Escapism, therefore, is par for the course,
A need for imaginative thinking in force,
A fantasy trip that can take us away,
And help us get through the routine of the day,
Everyone does it; we all have to dream,
However unlikely our thinking may seem,
And though we're aware that our dreams *can't* come true,
We carry on dreaming that one day they do,
I'm stuck in a wheelchair; I'm feeling so ill,
I've had it - I'm finished, but in my head still,
I've not given up on the dreams in my mind,
Reality's something that's best left behind,
I *still* think I'll be a huge rock 'n' roll star,
I'll be the world's greatest footballer by far,
I'll be the most popular person on Earth,
There'll be a bank holiday marking my birth,
I'll conquer world poverty; heal all the sick,
I'll make Stephen Hawking look hopelessly thick,
I'm craving the day all these things are in place,
And having Miss World sitting close to my face,
We have to have dreams 'cause reality sucks,
Without them we're making ourselves sitting ducks,
To bouts of depression and feelings of woe,
We have to have dreams to escape what we know,
So rather than give way to truthful intrusion,
It's better creating a world of illusion,
The power of the mind helps us all to survive,
And dreaming is something worth keeping alive.

Graham Eastaugh 26/10/01

# Unlucky numbers

Angelica loved me; she gave me her heart,
She pledged that the two of us never would part,
She told me she worshipped me twenty-four seven,
Each three sixty-five till we both be in heaven,
She said a more gorgeous man she'd never met,
Insisting more lucky a girl couldn't get,
Whatever I did I was truly a dream,
She felt like the cat who had captured the cream,
She simply adored every word that I spoke,
She called me a ten out of ten of a bloke,
Describing my bedroom technique as ideal,
A lover who overflowed raw sex appeal,
She said I was great; absolutely the best,
She said I was light years ahead of the rest,
She worshipped me twenty-four seven she said,
Each three sixty-five till the day she was dead,
But just as my love life seemed fully secure,
A shock to my system I had to endure,
One February night, on the twenty-ninth day,
She cut off my goolies and threw them away,
I couldn't believe the deceit she'd displayed,
Betraying the pledges of love that she'd made,
I told her I'd never felt quite so beguiled,
"How many days in a leap year?" she smiled.

Graham Eastaugh 10/10/01

# Wacky races

Cowboys were goodies, and Indians bad,
Though palefaces stole all that Indians had,
Non-whites were simply inferior souls,
And black people lived out subservient roles,
I have to be honest; a long time ago,
I saw this as just, for I just didn't know,
For that's how the TV presented the 'facts',
To question the screen was the foulest of acts,
With each generation, opinions change,
The bigotry lessens, and views rearrange,
The reason's quite simple in my estimation,
The answers all lie in improved education,
It's really quite strange how a thought can begin,
That someone is judged by the shade of their skin,
How some people hold such an arrogant mind,
Believing themselves of superior kind,
But over the years, things can only improve,
As long as our learning curve keeps on the move,
And who knows? There might come a time in the game,
We finally realise we're all just the same?

Graham Eastaugh 18/2/00

# Nothing but the truth

When I was fifteen; still a pupil at school,
I had no idea of my future at all,
I hadn't a thought on a chosen career,
The prospect of work only filled me with fear,
My headmaster told me I'd have to think twice,
And booked an appointment to get some advice,
I sat at a table with someone called Bob,
And hoped he could find me a suitable job,
We talked about hobbies, and things I enjoyed,
He asked me what things made me greatly annoyed,
I told him my pastimes were croquet and swimming,
The things that annoyed me were paupers and women,
I couldn't stand females who dressed to attract,
Then sounded surprised when they then got attacked,
My views on the matter were quite unreserved,
That some of those women got what they deserved,
I told him I never kept up with the news,
And didn't like people with working-class views,
I liked a good drink among well-spoken crowds,
And spent half my life with my head in the clouds,
The futures adviser was shaking his head,
He didn't agree with a word that I'd said,
He said I was foolish, but bore me no grudge,
Then asked if I'd thought of becoming a judge.

Graham Eastaugh 1/10/99

# Personally speaking

I've always been proud of the language I use,
I speak in plain English when airing my views,
I say what I mean, and leave no one in doubt,
So everyone knows what I'm talking about,
But not everybody has diction like me,
As some ways of talking and mine don't agree,
For some people talk in a different way,
And go to great lengths to disguise what they say,
I went out to lunch a few Sundays ago,
Just me and a beautiful woman I know,
We went to a restaurant; ordered a meal,
But some of the things that she said were unreal,
I felt so confused by the wording she chose,
She said she was going to powder her nose,
She walked from the table; I blew her a kiss,
And said: "While you're there, you can stop for a piss,"
She didn't return for a few minutes more,
And told me the state of her stomach was poor,
She said that she'd spent so much time in the loo,
Because she had tried for a quick number two,
I gave some advice which I said she should heed,
And whispered: "A really good shit's what you need,"
She then said her back passage needed repair,
I told her I'd find a good builder somewhere,
She then said she had a confession to make,
And said she was sorry my heart she would break,
She told me most nights she still sleeps with her ex,
I answered: "As long as you're not having sex,"
I find it quite strange an intelligent race,
Can find it so hard putting words into place,
You might find my language a trifle obscene,
But my way of living's to say what I mean.

Graham Eastaugh 13/5/01

# A very peculiar practice

Remember, remember, the fifth of November,
It's more like a case of: how can we forget?
They start selling fireworks in early September,
To celebrate quelling a terrorist threat,
But hold on a moment. What's going on here?
Just why do these crass celebrations survive?
We go through the same rigmarole every year,
For something that happened in 1605,
I know it's good fun to watch firework displays,
Despite the fact fireworks can cost such a lot,
But think of the way Guy Fawkes spent his last days,
Repaying his debt for the Gunpowder Plot,
Imprisoned and tortured, he waited to die,
His plan for destruction was fatally thwarted,
A massive crowd gathered; the hangman stood by,
And then he was brutally hanged, drawn and quartered,
Now call me old-fashioned, a killjoy maybe,
But how can we cheer something gruesome like that?
Consider the facts, and I think you'll agree,
That's no way to die, for not even a rat,
A civilised race shouldn't celebrate death,
It's far more humane to mourn somebody's loss,
We'd never commemorate terminal breath,
Of someone who died being nailed to a cross.

Graham Eastaugh 23/6/99

# Those were the days

Our school days were truly the best of our lives,
Well, everyone's frequently telling me so,
It's hard to believe how the myth still survives,
Or am I alone in my thoughts? I don't know,
The way I remember them, times weren't so grand,
I worked in the day, and at night-time as well,
I ended each week with no cash in my hand,
And lived every hour by a stupid school bell,
I had to be quiet, and I had to sit still,
While most of the teachers would fill me with dread,
And most days for lunch I was eating pigswill,
And if I had fun, I got whacked round the head,
I stayed in detention for hundreds of hours,
My arse the headmaster would violently flog,
I picked up verrucas in freezing cold showers,
And sometimes my head would get flushed down the bog,
So were those days *really* the best that we've had?
We've never had better, not since or before?
Or maybe I'm wrong, and those times weren't so bad?
But if they're the best, then the rest are piss-poor.

Graham Eastaugh 16/6/99

# Words about turds

It started as plip-plop, and then became pooh,
And following pooh it became number two,
The next evolutionary step of the word,
Was leaving the abacus, changing to turd,
And then a bit later I opted to plump,
For having a crap, which evolved into dump,
Each one of these terms at the time was a hit,
And these days I'm perfectly happy with shit,
We've so many words that all mean the same thing,
And as we get older the changes we ring,
It wouldn't sound right to be dumping at three,
And forty-year-olds having plops shouldn't be,
Whatever we call it, it's always the same,
The texture or smell doesn't change with the name,
Excreta or faeces, a motion or stool,
The truth is the name doesn't matter at all,
It isn't important what wording we use,
We all do the same so there's nothing to lose,
As anyone knows of particular class,
The only important thing's wiping your arse.

Graham Eastaugh 25/12/01

# Something in the air

I travelled up north just the other weekend,
In order to visit a very old friend,
Our paths hadn't crossed for a number of years,
I thought we should meet for a couple of beers,
I knocked on his door, then I tidied my hair,
And thought of the tales from the past we could share,
The door slowly opened, and brimming with glee,
I said to his lovely wife: "Doris, it's me!"
"It's you!" she exclaimed, not believing her eyes,
"I thought you were dead; what a lovely surprise."
She welcomed me in, and her husband she called,
Then Arthur walked in looking greatly enthralled,
He gave me a hug, and we shook hands as well,
It's then that I noticed this terrible smell,
The air in the room was incredibly thick,
I gagged and was feeling uncomfortably sick,
"Arthur," I said, "have you just shit yourself?
'Cause if not you're in the most terrible health."
He laughed out aloud, and he said: "You daft sod,
You must think of me as remarkably odd."
"He is," said his wife, "'cause that hideous stink,
Is nothing to do with my spouse like you think,
It's our Christmas present from Seamus and Flo,
The one that we got from them ten years ago,
A lovely Alsatian called Shergar it was,
And, though he's now dead, he still keeps him because..."
Then Arthur piped up, interrupting his wife:
"They're not just for Christmas - a dog is for life."

Graham Eastaugh 24/7/09

# Relatively outrageous

It pains me to say so, but long in my past,
The way I behaved could be sometimes obscene,
Aware that forever my youth wouldn't last,
I put it about, if you know what I mean,
And one of the nightclubs I used to frequent,
Played host to my social requirements just right,
Each Tuesday it suited my sexual intent,
By staging an evening called 'grab-a-gran' night,
I'd go there each week with a good friend or two,
And always be armed with an honest week's wage,
I'd drink lots of beers, then with little ado,
I'd pick up a woman of more mature age,
One night I remember ahead of the rest,
My conquest that evening was treated like dirt,
Respect for my elders was not at its best,
My only concern was a 'score' to convert,
The acts I performed on that woman were gross,
To me she was nothing but meat for my lust,
It's little surprise she was rendered morose,
I'd left in the night in a state of disgust,
I'd realised I knew her and now wanted out,
I felt quite appalled at the things I had done,
It frightened me shitless without any doubt,
Reality dawned and it wasn't much fun,
And now, in the present, I'm full of remorse,
Though, in my defence, it was not only me,
The women were there to meet fellas, of course,
And ladies aged forty or more got in free,
She later forgave me and shouldered the blame,
Though she said I'd been somewhat simplistic,
She hugged me and said I should suffer no shame,
But my granddad went fucking ballistic.

Graham Eastaugh 13/9/02

# Trading places

Look me in the eye, and then explain exactly why,
You think it such a mournful fate to prematurely die,
When quality of life has disappeared with years gone by,
And dreams of future happiness distinctly don't apply,
And tell me with your hand on heart if I were you instead,
That optimistic thoughts would freely flow within your head,
That every trace of hopelessness was simply put to bed,
And fear forever gripped you at the thought of being dead,
And study the reflection in the mirror on the wall,
Then answer this: if I were you would life be such a ball,
With tortured mind and broken body only fit to fall,
And ever less reserves of inner strength on which to call?
My guess is you would take the view my life holds scant appeal,
An arduous existence in a far from perfect deal,
Of course, imagination's not the same as life for real,
But think of me as you instead and tell me how *you'd* feel.

Graham Eastaugh 11/11/07

# Going for a song

Tina and Marge are a couple of tarts,
I've known since a long time ago,
A night at a Chinky's where this story starts,
The following picture unravelled like so:
Tina and Marge and I each took a seat,
And started to burst into song,
We sang like a dream with an excellent beat,
But got all the words to the song titles wrong,
The waiter come over; we ordered some food,
He loved all the songs that we'd sung,
The grub soon arrived, but I felt in a mood,
'Cause they'd given us *too much foo yung*,
I said to the waiter: *"Don't peeve me this way,*
I ordered a mini, not maxi,
Selection of foo yung, so take this away,"
And gave him a kick up his *big yellow jacksy*,
I spotted a fit Rastafarian sort,
I got up and sat by her side,
But, sadly, her husband's attention I caught,
However, a different tactic I tried,
I said to the bloke: *"Shave your missus for me,*
As surely us both she can please?"
A *black tragic woman* she turned out to be,
As she had a distasteful venereal disease,
Her husband said: "Go on then, do what you like,"
"A condom," I said, "I've not got,"
"No problem," he said, and I said: "On your bike,
Because condomless shagging your missus I'm not,"
He said: "Are you sure?" I said: "No doubt about it,
I don't want a nasty discharge,
*I don't want to pork,"* I insisted, *"without it,"*
Then I wandered away back to Tina and Marge,
We settled the bill, but so pissed we'd become,
We hadn't a brain cell between us,
The bill was a most *indivisible sum*,
And I was in charge of an unemployed penis,

Tina and Marge said I looked rather sad,
And sported a sorry demeanour,
I told them the night was the best that I'd had,
And so *don't cry for me Marge 'n' Tina.*

Graham Eastaugh 25/3/01

# All the fun of the fair

When I was a kid I would sometimes feel down,
But always cheered up when the fair came to town,
They'd come here for weeks in the park every year,
I always perked up when the funfair was here,
I loved the whole atmosphere - music and lights,
I'd save all my money and go there most nights,
It satisfied all my inquisitive ways,
Those without question at all were the days,
I'd always get candyfloss stuck in my hair,
And see someone getting a kicking somewhere,
I'd win the odd coconut, much to my pride,
Later to find out it's rotten inside,
I'd whirl on the waltzer and lose my loose change,
My nose might be threatened to be rearranged,
I'd throw plastic darts, and my money away,
The goldfish I won always died the next day,
I'd win useless prizes too cheap to be true,
And buy greasy hamburgers too tough to chew,
I'd ride on the Dodgems to sounds from the charts,
And watch phoney Gypsies oblige the young tarts,
Those days at the fair I assure you were great,
Nothing around at the time could equate,
But looking back now, if those days were the best,
I'm glad I can barely remember the rest.

Graham Eastaugh 24/11/01

# All's well that ends well

This is the tale of Catastrophe Jack,
A person who had the most unhappy knack,
Of finding himself in positions of woe,
His luck was appalling wherever he'd go,
His wife looked exactly the same as Geoff Capes,
He owned only Betamax video tapes,
His daughter was just like his wife, but more manly,
The team he supported was Accrington Stanley,
Wherever calamity loomed he'd arrive,
He jointly invented the Sinclair C5,
He owned a small holiday home in Kabul,
Of BSE-infected meat he was full,
He slept with a girl who was dying of Aids,
When diamonds were trumps he would only have spades,
He wasn't too sharp in his business affairs,
He'd thousands of ITV Digital shares,
He once had a bet that the world would soon end,
Osama bin Laden was once his best friend,
He dismally failed with each target he set,
His only success was in Russian roulette,
And that's how he perished - his brains on the floor,
His life was a tale of misfortune, for sure,
But though all he touched turned to shit in the main,
At least he can't be so unlucky again.

Graham Eastaugh 27/3/02

# Beyond belief

The little girl sat on her grandmother's knee,
And asked for the umpteenth time: "How can it be,
That so many people are dying from Aids,
While other folk perish in military raids?
And how come some people don't have enough food,
Yet others have wealth that would seem almost crude?
And why should it be our environment's doomed,
And not ever perfect like once we'd assumed?"
Her grandmother answered: "That's just how it is,
God pulls all the strings; the decisions are His,
You've possibly heard the familiar phrase,
That God sometimes moves in mysterious ways,"
"But, surely, Grandmother," the little girl said,
"He's able to make things much better instead,
He holds all the cards and, I guess, is no fool,
So how come he's not taking care of us all?"
The little girl's grandmother couldn't explain,
And told her to not ask such questions again,
She found her persistence uncomfortably odd,
And told her to not doubt the wisdom of God,
The little girl then went to bed up the stairs,
Her grandmother said: "Don't forget...say your prayers,"
The little girl, just before saying 'good night',
Said: "Grandmother, stop talking absolute shite."

Graham Eastaugh 6/7/07

156

# Great expectations

It's hard not to notice how certain things change,
Behavioural patterns that strike us as strange,
How some groups are bringing tradition to end,
By bucking the stereotypical trend,
The people in question are women and girls,
They're ditching their image of ribbons and curls,
They're sick of behaving all girlish and nice,
They're no longer acting like sugar and spice,
It's hard to believe, but not *that* long ago,
A woman was 'property', only for show,
They had to be dainty, and look really cute,
They shouldn't get drunk, and they had to be mute,
But times are a-changing; they're now getting pissed,
And starting a fight's ever hard to resist,
They're piercing their nipples, and having tattoos,
They're going to football, and wearing blokes' shoes,
But why is it shocking they're acting like this?
It's only an image that's going amiss,
It could be an instance of envy, perhaps,
That, suddenly, girls are behaving like chaps?
I can't really say that I'm shocked to the core,
This kind of example we've all seen before,
Of people rejecting the label they've got,
Forever desiring to be what they're 'not',
There once was a time when a man was a man,
When anyone worthy would do all he can,
To shelter his feelings, and keep them inside,
To cry would portray an effeminate side,
But look at things now, there's a whole change of heart,
A bloke is *encouraged* to act like a tart,
Those views from the old days have all disappeared,
Now, if you're not camp you're considered as weird,
We'd all like to be what we actually aren't,

We'd like to be somebody else, but we can't,
I guess it's quite natural these thoughts should take shape,
We all have our moments of longed for escape,
We're pressured to act a particular way,
Whatever's expected, we're urged to obey,
To be individual is almost a sin,
And that's why the bulk of us choose to blend in.

Graham Eastaugh 15/3/00

# Age concern

The old woman undressed and thought of her past,
The state of her body had left her aghast,
The mirror reflected a vision of truth,
She pined for the days when she still had her youth,
She smiled rather wryly when turning back time,
Her mind going back to the days of her prime,
She thought it ironic how things should pan out,
Her early teens what she was thinking about,
She pictured herself as considerably bolder,
Recalling she always desired to look older,
She now thought it foolish, but wasn't to blame,
As each of her friends was exactly the same,
She thought of the evenings of padded-out bras,
And make-up galore to gain access to bars,
She thought of the cigarettes; staying out late,
Remembering how growing up couldn't wait,
With hindsight she saw it as utterly mad,
Betraying the childhood she yesteryear had,
How now she was old, she would *love* to be young,
She couldn't work out how that phase was unsung,
She sat and berated her arthritic pains,
While glumly surveying her varicose veins,
She stared at the shelf where her wedding snap sits,
The days when she didn't have sad, saggy tits,
She mourned for her youth; how she'd wished it away,
Her pubic enclosure all wiry and grey,
Abdominal muscles alarmingly slack,
And something unsightly somewhere round the back,
It's weird how we want to be different ages,
We want to flick forward or back a few pages,
We tackle most issues without too much fuss,
But rarely content ourselves just being us.

Graham Eastaugh 27/5/01

# My way of thinking

The wood was deserted; the atmosphere still,
A group of us naked, awaiting the kill,
We stood in a circle, and looked to the sky,
Our object of sacrifice ready to die,
The rest of the people I'd not met before,
I wasn't prepared for the huge shock in store,
It soon became midnight; we started to chant,
Proceedings then took on a sinister slant,
We worshipped the devil; a chicken came out,
Its brutal beheading was then brought about,
We then had an orgy, and rolled in the mud,
Then took turns in drinking the dead chicken's blood,
It's then that I found myself feeling a fool,
Our worshipping hadn't been earnest at all,
A little man jumped out and laughed as he said,
"Gotcha!" And anger transformed my face red,
"Edmonds, you arsehole!" I shouted aloud,
Much to the shock of the rest of the crowd,
They thought it was funny; I thought it was not,
I showed them the passion for vengeance I'd got,
His idea of humour and mine don't agree,
I thus strung the little shit up from a tree,
From now on we should see much less of the prat,
And all should be ever so grateful for that.

Graham Eastaugh 13/7/01

# More than a woman

I remember my time in the Far East so well,
It gave me the following story to tell,
A harrowing tale if the truth should be told,
A memory of Thailand to turn my flesh cold,
I'd gone on my own just to travel around,
With purely the aim of exploring new ground,
I saw all the sights, and I had a great time,
On top of that Mount Fujiyama I'd climb,
But after a while I was bored on my own,
One part of my body was craving a home,
I had a few drinks; then I had a few more,
Then went about finding myself a cheap whore,
With hindsight it's obvious I drank a bit much,
In calming my nerves for a prostitute's touch,
But that's how it was as I set up the deal,
For ending this spell of frustration I'd feel,
We went to a room with a huge double bed,
She told me she'd willingly do what I said,
I fully undressed; then I took off her bra,
Her tits were the biggest I'd witnessed by far,
We fumbled about and it's then things turned sour,
This certainly wasn't my conquering hour,
My hand felt a penis; my stomach felt sick,
I'd lost all the feeling I had in my dick!
I suddenly realised it wasn't my tool,
I'd not lost my intimate senses at all,
So being quite brainy, I came up with this:
The knob wasn't mine, so it must have been *his*!
I ran for the door as I'd never felt worse,
I'd found myself struck by the ladyboy curse,
The fact I'd been fooled was undoubtedly weird,
Though maybe I should have suspected the beard?

Graham Eastaugh 17/1/02

# Keeping up appearances

"Without any doubt, there's nowt like a trout,
With both of her mammary glands hanging out,"
The Yorkshireman said to his drinking pal, Fred,
Who'd rather be out with his whippets instead,
But Arthur was quite an intolerant chap,
And festered with rage underneath his flat cap,
He ordered his twelfth round of drinks of the day,
Declaring the fact he was too tight to pay,
He lived on black pudding, but couldn't stand Blacks,
And carried out numerous racist attacks,
He idolised Illingworth, Trueman and Close,
And judged homosexual behaviour as gross,
Such venomous bigotry spewed from his mouth,
Detesting all people who came from 'down south',
He did what he bloody well liked in his life,
Believing all 'women's work' jobs for the wife,
The barmaid was born in a Hertfordshire town,
And branded old Arthur an ignorant clown,
She said he belonged in Neanderthal times,
Describing his viewpoints as cerebral crimes,
"You Cockneys know bugger all," Arthur replied,
Believing quite firmly he'd right on his side,
He said he was sorry for talking such tripe,
"But that's how it is with a stereotype."

Graham Eastaugh 19/12/07

# Time

The pain was so much I'd have happily died,
I tried to stay calm but was screaming inside,
The hands of the clock seemed impossibly slow,
As if to compound my position of woe,
The whole situation seemed somewhat surreal,
How time passed more slowly the worse I would feel,
I stared at the clock on the wall in dismay,
An hour took so long it felt more like a day,
This state of affairs left me greatly annoyed,
For time went so fast doing things I enjoyed,
I'd always thought time was consistent in pace,
But now I'd discovered this *wasn't* the case,
A day in the office can seem like a year,
A lunch break, however, can soon disappear,
And time in a traffic jam always drags on,
While holidays come but so quickly have gone,
Time tends to stand still when the going gets tough,
A much-needed sleep never lasts long enough,
The month of November feels longer than June,
And how many people think sex ends too soon?
But, generally speaking, time travels so fast,
The present, in no time at all, is the past,
And one of these days when we're all past our prime,
We'll all come to realise we've run out of time.

Graham Eastaugh 18/10/09

# Not bloody likely!

A Member of Parliament being sincere,
A Tannoy announcement that's perfectly clear,
A child being born to its 'mother', a man,
A black person joining the Ku Klux Klan,
An A&E ward having nothing to do,
A boy band or girl group that does something new,
An Englishman wearing the Wimbledon crown,
A knob in a porn film that *always* stays down,
A middle-aged woman who doesn't like Des,
A salesman who *really* believes what he says,
A world in which *everyone* has equal rights,
A British kebab shop that never has fights,
The way of the world always strikes me as strange,
We all like to think we can bring about change,
But some things in life are inflexible tracts,
A series of most inescapable facts,
As certain things stand, that's the way that they'll stay,
It's best to accept that they're staying that way,
There *can't* be a thing such as life after death,
I might be mistaken, but don't hold your breath.

Graham Eastaugh 17/5/01

# From zero to hero

Religion is something I don't understand,
With all the conflicting beliefs in the land,
How one group of people see their faith as true,
While others may take an alternative view,
The thing that persistently baffles me most?
The Catholic faith and its premier post,
I mean no offence, not a solitary word,
But isn't the Pope situation absurd?
He starts out in life as a total unknown,
Wherever he travels, he's left well alone,
He can't save the world, or indeed offer hope,
But everything changes the day he's named Pope,
He's held in the most unbelievable awe,
But I, for one, don't know exactly what for,
I find all the mass adulation a joke,
Apart from the name, he's an ordinary bloke,
He wasn't a talented rock and roll star,
He didn't teach Hendrix to play the guitar,
He didn't play sport, or appear on TV,
He just lived a humble life like you and me,
The way he's so idolised strikes me as odd,
Each day of his life he gets treated like God,
So what could have happened to make him so blessed?
The way he's received, you would think he's George Best,
With no special skills, he's achieved global fame,
He gained his appeal just by changing his name,
And when his time's over, there's nothing to lose,
There'll always be someone to step in his shoes.

Graham Eastaugh 25/6/99

# Something stupid

Roger and Hector were very good pals,
While Susan and Dawn were the gentlemen's gals,
They made up a foursome of utter delight,
But everything changed on a midsummer night,
Hector got drunk before rogering Sue,
But Roger refused to believe this was true,
Till Dawn said the reason he'd rogered his wife,
Was Roger had hectored poor Sue all her life,
It suddenly dawned on him what he had done,
By hectoring Sue to another she'd run,
Dawn then informed Hector she'd sue for divorce,
While Hector declared he was full of remorse,
Roger then promised he'd hector no more,
While Hector regretted he'd rogered before,
Dawn's threat to sue for divorce was withdrawn,
While Sue hoped the whole thing was not a false dawn,
So Roger and Hector were good friends again,
And Sue and Dawn quickly forgot all their pain,
The four of them said they'd forgiveness to thank,
Though, none of them really exists, to be frank.

Graham Eastaugh 3/8/09

# In sickness and in health

I was deep in the mire without any doubt,
While up a gumtree with my knob hanging out,
It seemed there was nothing to do except pray,
And hope all my troubles would soon go away,
I'd found myself based on a hospital ward,
With pain in both legs as my temperature soared,
However, despite this position of strife,
I somehow acquired a new outlook on life,
Some veterans I met of the Second World War,
Each one with humility deep to the core,
They'd fought to ensure that their country stayed free,
And passed on the bounty to people like me,
I also met numerous medical staff,
Who'd chosen to tread a philanthropist's path,
They each displayed selflessness straight from the heart,
And all had that something that set them apart,
These two groups of people had opened my eyes,
Though, frankly, they shouldn't have caused such surprise,
The lesson they'd taught me I'd learnt long ago,
That life's about substance and not merely show,
Integrity, here, is the name of the game,
And content of character likewise the same,
I knew in life what really mattered or not,
It's just through the years I quite crassly forgot,
My spell of ill-health was a huge wake-up call,
I needed a kick up the backside, that's all,
The following thought-process then came to pass:
I'd spent so much time with my head up my arse,
I've learnt to be grateful for each little thing,
To milk the enjoyment small mercies can bring,
So much over time with my body's gone wrong,
At least my appendix is still going strong.

Graham Eastaugh 24/7/09

# Straight talking

"All right?" said the man walking by in the street,
So I stopped and then answered: "Not really,"
The man kept on walking with fast-moving feet,
For his question was asked insincerely,
I ran to confront him, I felt so irate,
And he said: "Don't get out of your pram!"
I said to the gentleman: "Listen here, mate,
Why ask if you don't give a toss how I am?"
"You can say that again," said the man with a smile,
So I did; then he told me to stop,
I counted to ten; bit my lip for a while,
I was so close to blowing my top,
"If you heard what I said," I then angrily said,
"Why the insistence on being a pain?
The words that I'd spoken went into your head,
So why bloody tell me to say them again?"
I said I was sorry for losing my cool,
And said I was stressed, and he answered me so:
"Tell me about it," and just like a fool,
I did, but he didn't a jot want to know,
My head blew a fuse; he was walking away,
And he didn't await my reply,
We so often don't mean a word that we say,
And we all know we do it. But why?

Graham Eastaugh 5/5/01

# Heroes and villains

We'd all like to be fondly thought of when gone,
To make an impression before passing on,
To have lots of people remember our name,
And, preferably, go down in life's hall of fame,
But look back through history, and if you're like me,
A who's who of good guys you likely won't see,
For yesterday's heroes get put in the shade,
By those who chose evil as *their* stock in trade,
We quickly forget all the good that's been done,
But everyone's heard of Attila the Hun,
And Hitler and Stalin, who killed such a lot,
And had he been kind, who'd have heard of Pol Pot?
Napoleon's famous all over the Earth,
But no one could claim he provided much mirth,
A callous dictator, he lived by the sword,
Yet all of his misdeeds are simply ignored,
We know well of Crippen, and Christie and Haigh,
But thoughts of philanthropists seem rather vague,
We've all heard of Sutcliffe, and someone called 'Jack',
Yet memories of heroes are something we lack,
So, if it's to live in the memory you crave,
You want to be thought of when long in your grave,
You want to go down in the annals of Man,
You'd better be evil as much as you can.

Graham Eastaugh 27/3/00

# Unsolved mysteries

Who built the pyramids? How were they built?
And why so much blood on our battlefields spilt?
How did the world begin? Why are we here?
And what is our future? And is the end near?
Who wrote the Bible? And should we obey?
And who fired the bullet that killed JFK?
What killed the dinosaurs? Is Elvis dead?
And who was the beast who brought Whitechapel dread?
Will cancerous growths soon be rendered benign?
Was Hurst's World Cup Final goal over the line?
Is life any better since Armstrong splashed down?
And was it immoral procuring von Braun?
Are governments feeding us misinformation?
And after we've gone is there reincarnation?
Does lager taste best from a bottle or keg?
And which appeared firstly, the chicken or egg?
I've so many questions, but answers so few,
I've plenty of theories, but which ones are true?
The harder I think I become more confused,
I'm left in the dark, and my ego is bruised,
I've never pretended to understand life,
There's many a puzzle to cause me such strife,
But the riddle that causes my brain most to throb,
Is why did my Action Man not have a knob?

Graham Eastaugh 17/10/99

# Fly-on-the-wall report

"I might as well die," said the bluebottle fly,
To another bluebottle one night,
The other bluebottle enquired as to why,
So the other one's views came to light,
"Be honest," he said, "we'd be better off dead,
As our lives are so tediously dull,
From morning till late, our existence ain't great,
As we're each of us out of our skull,
It's boring, that's what, this crap lifestyle we've got,
I detest with my heart every bit,
We've nothing to do, except trample in pooh,
As our reason for living is shit,
We live on the stuff; we just can't get enough,
So wherever a turd is, we're there,
When crap's on the street, we persistently meet,
And whatever's on offer we share,
We're seen as a pest, and we never get rest,
As we always get ushered away,
Wherever we land, we're attacked by a hand,
And we're never invited to stay."
The other bluebottle, his name Aristotle,
Responded in kind as he sat,
"I see what you mean, that our life's not a dream,"
Then a newspaper squashed them both flat.

Graham Eastaugh 29/4/01

# Luck be a lady?

If luck be a lady, then what be a man?
I'll try to examine the facts if I can,
I don't know if anyone tends to agree,
But ladies appear quite *un*lucky to me,
They don't have the physical strength that men do,
Whatever their figure, it's something they rue,
The fact it's a man's world can quell their ambition,
They can't have a piss in a standing position,
Whenever they cry they're 'emotional wrecks',
They're labelled as slappers for enjoying sex,
Their most private part periodically bleeds,
They pay a lot more for their underwear needs,
For toilet trips publicly queuing's required,
They have to bear children if kids are desired,
And childbirth has plenty of hardship in store,
Like squeezing a grape through a small drinking straw,
So luck be a lady? I hardly think so,
They seem to have more than their fair share of woe,
The saying that luck be a lady's a joke,
If luck be a lady, then what be a bloke?

Graham Eastaugh 26/9/02

# Food for thought

If alien beings should visit our world,
I wonder what chain of events would unfurl?
And more to the point, would they come here in peace?
Or would all known human existence soon cease?
As things stand at present, we're masters of all,
Of all living creatures, we're top in the school,
But were things to change, and invasion take place,
Just how would we fare as a second-class race?
The way I see things, we'd be living in dread,
And crossing our fingers they don't want us dead,
And hoping they're not in belligerent mood,
And, most of all, praying they bring their own food,
For each single life form inhabiting Earth,
Each part of the world sees a differing worth,
A dog has a great life, though not in Korea,
An Israeli pig has got nothing to fear,
An Indian cow has a much-revered stance,
A frog's on the hop if residing in France,
There's many a conflicting viewpoint to note,
And who'd like to be a West Indian goat?
We humans are so used to playing at king,
But one day invasion might change everything,
We'd play second fiddle, and all feel displaced,
And pray that we're not to an alien's taste.

Graham Eastaugh 16/1/00

# Different class

The class system doesn't exist any more,
And everyone's equal like never before,
But I'm not convinced, though they tell me it's true,
Then memories of yesteryear came into view,
I'll tell you a tale of a marquess's daughter,
We used to live close; then I started to court her,
We never got on almost right from the start,
Our different backgrounds were so far apart,
She lived in a mansion; I lived in the gutter,
I used to eat lard, whereas she would eat butter,
I had a pet rat she considered as coarse,
While she owned a champion thoroughbred horse,
Her upper-class accent would drive me bananas,
She spent all her weekends attending gymkhanas,
She drove a Rolls-Royce, while I travelled on foot,
And she enjoyed caviar; I endured soot,
Her dad had a butler he ordered around,
His gardener tended to acres of ground,
And priceless antiques decorated his house,
Each August the twelfth he'd go shooting for grouse,
So don't talk to me about being the same,
I've never heard such a ridiculous claim,
For such a suggestion's an absolute farce,
The class system isn't existent, my arse!

Graham Eastaugh 18/10/99

# Tall stories

Drake, he played bowls as he watched the Armada,
Samson brought death when he pushed pillars harder,
Richard III offered all for a horse,
Goliath was felled by a slingshot, of course,
"Let them eat cake," said Marie Antoinette,
Rasputin enchanted all women he met,
Napoleon said: "Not tonight, Josephine,"
Victoria wasn't a much-amused queen,
Nero, he fiddled while watching Rome burn,
And Whittington followed when summoned to turn,
Nelson requested from Hardy a kiss,
And Jesus Christ chose to give swimming a miss,
History thrills me, with tales from the past,
How every small detail we know to the last,
We think that's the case, but I'm not quite so sure,
The chance it's all phoney is hard to ignore,
I feel it's more likely from Antoinette's tongue,
The words really uttered were 'Let them eat dung,'
And Drake wasn't bowling, as tutored in schools,
He spotted some Spaniards, and simply said 'Balls!'
I'd love to believe all the stories I've heard,
That all things recorded are true, every word,
I hope all the history of sport gets cocked up,
It's England's best chance of a second World Cup.

Graham Eastaugh 12/1/00

# Return to sender

Beam me up, Scotty: I'm done with this place,
I'm sick of this two-bit incompetent race,
I've been here five decades fart-arsing about,
I gave it my best shot, and now I want out,
My mission's completed; it's time to return,
There's nothing I don't know of humans to learn,
The creatures on Earth aren't the same as I thought,
I hereby submit my concluding report:
They go round in circles with minimal fun,
And most of them never get anything done,
Their sense of perspective is frightfully poor,
The things they excel at are hatred and war,
Their values revolve around image and wealth,
And one trait they all have in common is stealth,
They strangely engender unnecessary stress,
And most of their lives are a terrible mess,
They don't seem to know how to utilise time,
And some of the sad bastards dabble in rhyme,
They're well beyond saving, so beam me up now,
I've seen all the shit that one life should allow,
And though for the most part I tried all I could,
I guess my appearance on Earth did no good,
So let's put my stay on this planet to bed,
I'd much rather be fighting Klingons instead.

Graham Eastaugh 29/3/02

# From here to eternity

A fanatical Islamic friend of mine,
Politely described his religion's design,
I listened intently while raising no doubt,
As Abdul explained what his faith was about,
He lectured me in the most passionate way,
How Allah was praised many times every day,
How women would partially cover the face,
How one month a year Ramadan is in place,
He wanted to know how I felt about death,
My thoughts of the future on terminal breath,
My views on the afterlife after I'm dead,
Religious beliefs that were held in my head,
I told him religion meant nothing to me,
Despite being registered once C of E,
I didn't believe in an afterlife mode,
The moment I die, that's the end of the road,
He told me that his was a different fate,
His kind had prosperity lying in wait,
When this life was over, it opened the door,
A much more enjoyable time was in store,
He spoke of a much better place he would go,
A life after death to enrapture him so,
Where numerous virgins would be at his call,
A truly magnificent fate to befall,
I gave lots of thought to the words that he spoke,
The different emotions his speech would evoke,
I thought on the one hand his views were absurd,
Yet fully respected the things that I'd heard,
How dead or alive he's got nothing to lose,
He wins either way with those afterlife views,
A much better life after death he attains,
So, being a good mate, I blew out his brains.

Graham Eastaugh 20/1/02

# Mother's pride

Over the years, in the course of my life,
I've come across many a mother and wife,
Who've one thing in common when all's said and done,
They've all got remarkable children bar none,
Each one of these kids is incredibly bright,
Whatever the question they'll always be right,
Their mothers insist they're unlike all the rest,
Their daughters and sons can compete with the best,
I've heard about daughters advanced for their years,
And sons for whom nothing perplexing appears,
How *everyone's* children are brighter than most,
How *every* child bears that particular boast,
Each child on the planet's the best it would seem,
For every mum thinks that her offspring's the cream,
We must have *some* idiots here where we live,
But not many mums call their 'baby' a div,
So there lies the answer - we're none of us fools,
As far as a mother's concerned they're the rules,
But if that's a fact without reasonable doubt,
Then how come we've so many dullards about?

Graham Eastaugh 21/5/01

# Internal inquiry

I went to the doctor's a few years ago,
Concerning a problem that troubled me so,
He told me to come in, and then get undressed,
And then to bend over, then he'd do the rest,
He put on a rubber glove; smeared it with grease,
And started to rub up and down in my crease,
He poked and he prodded, inspecting my skin,
And then, with a judder, his finger went in,
The finger came out, then he had a close look,
An hour and a half all this rigmarole took,
He handled my goolies, then told me to cough,
Then one of his trouser fly buttons flew off,
The telephone rang, so I put on my jeans,
He told me to carry on eating my greens,
To drink a bit less, and to exercise more,
To drink lots of water, and eat my steak raw,
Now don't think I'm being a little unfair,
But something to me seemed a bit fishy there,
'Cause seven days later, I chose to go back,
And found to my shock he'd been given the sack,
But here's why I think he was suspect, you see,
It wasn't his way of examining me,
It wasn't the time my consultancy took,
I'd only popped in there to borrow a book.

Graham Eastaugh 7/8/01

# What difference does it make?

We're told it's the end of the world as we know it,
We've one final chance and we'd better not blow it,
Our planet is clinging to life by a thread,
It's time to take action or finish up dead,
The icecaps are melting; sea levels are rising,
We're burning more fuel, so it's hardly surprising,
That polar bears find themselves treading thin ice,
And driving a 4 x 4 comes at a price,
We've too many aeroplanes high in the sky,
We have to act *now* or we're all gonna die,
The state of the ozone layer worsens each day,
We're throwing our grandchildren's futures away,
Our carbon emissions have gone through the roof,
The change in our climate bears palpable proof,
We need to recycle much more of our waste,
And have to find green issues more to our taste,
Forget about heaven, we're heading for hell,
We're using the wrong kind of light bulbs as well,
And just when I think I can't take any more,
I'm hearing a doomsday report from Al Gore,
But like every story, this tale has two sides,
And theories can quite often change with the tides,
And that's why I don't give a monkey's, you see,
It sounds like a load of old cobblers to me.

Graham Eastaugh  26/12/09

# Harsh lessons

I thought of my school days while sitting alone,
And tried to recall all the people I've known,
Above all the bulk of my thinking returned,
To all my tuition and things that I learned,
My schooling began at a very young age,
Twelve years of my life would this practice engage,
And now I look back on those formative years,
A list of the things I was taught reappears,
I learned about all sorts of things of no use,
Like whether an angle's acute or obtuse,
I learned about pi, and Pythagorus too,
While Shakespeare was simply too drab to be true,
We did nothing modern in history class,
Religious instruction was mythical farce,
The science lab offered an odious stench,
I learned how to ask for an apple in French,
Geography lessons were dull on the whole,
Like studying maps to see where we mine coal,
None of this stuff seems to get me too far,
I learned how to twang Alice Twattersby's bra,
I'm now nearly fifty and know a few things,
It's mostly the knowledge maturity brings,
I've reached the conclusion my twelve years at school,
In terms of much usefulness taught me sod all.

Graham Eastaugh 8/5/01

# The land of make-believe

Assuming that most other kids were like me,
I can't quite believe just how stupid were we,
In falling for some of the tales we were told,
By adults who'd keep certain knowledge on hold,
I must have been so unbelievably thick,
Believing as gospel each cruelly-played trick,
Whatever I heard, I considered as true,
I didn't raise doubts as I nowadays do,
How could I possibly think that some bloke,
Could fit through a pot built for letting out smoke?
And thinking about it, a worse thought appears:
We'd had central heating for nine or ten years!
The tooth fairy, pixies - I fell for it all,
I must have been some sort of half-witted fool,
I never envisaged these stories as odd,
At one time I even believed there's a God,
Unicorns, dragons - I thought they were real,
At no point a gullible git I would feel,
Although all these yarns I was spun were absurd,
I took them all in, and believed every word,
But not any more; I've a mind of my own,
I think for myself, as my writing has shown,
I'm now off to bed, but I'll keep on the light,
The bogeyman's coming to get me tonight.

Graham Eastaugh 5/6/01

# The riddle of the arts

I fully appreciate artistic skill,
A painting that's more than just run-of-the-mill,
I'm no connoisseur; just an ordinary bloke,
But isn't the art world a bit of a joke?
It's not only paintings, but sculpture as well,
It's hard to imagine how some of them sell,
Some things on show are, at best, rather nice,
But sell for a quite astronomical price,
Pablo Picasso is hailed as a great,
And Van Gogh is someone you love or you hate,
And Salvador Dali's a much-lauded chap,
But isn't his work just a load of old crap?
Their stuff sells for millions, but they're not to blame,
A painting is valued on nothing but name,
If Rembrandt had painted a canvas all black,
Then someone would buy it for gold by the sack,
It's all about snobbery; not about class,
The whole world of art's an embarrassing farce,
Sculpture's the same; there's some rubbish around,
Where everyday things sell for thousands of pounds,
I have my own sculpture; I made it last week,
It's Jeremy Clarkson, unable to speak,
His head's been detached and impaled on a spike,
It might not be art, but I know what I like.

Graham Eastaugh 24/6/99

# Nuff respect?

I'm quite a deep thinker on life in the main,
I try to imagine another one's pain,
In war situations of decades gone by,
Where rules of sheer horror grotesquely apply,
I think even more on Remembrance Day,
By brushing the cobwebs of history away,
The thoughts of those people who lived through it all,
The sorrowful memories they're bound to recall,
I wonder if anger prevails in their thoughts,
That so much is lost in this cruellest of 'sports',
The void they must feel that *we* don't have a clue,
Of anything any of them were put through,
They fought for their freedom - it had to be done,
Their daughters' and sons' future liberty won,
Their sense of perspective unwillingly gained,
The nightmares of warfare forever retained,
I wonder if now, in the present, they feel,
That modern existence is almost surreal,
Do kids of today have the life they deserve?
And is this the world that they fought to preserve?

Graham Eastaugh 11/11/01

184

# Terms of endearment

"Monkey, want some peanuts?" I said to my chum,
As I stood at the bar of the Kettle & Drum,
A woman walked over and called me a name,
Then gave me a slap in the face for my shame,
I couldn't believe her distinct lack of charm,
And told her I'd done nothing causing her harm,
She said: "Yes, you have. It's the wording you used,
Your black friend was racially cruelly abused."
"What are you talking about, you old trout?"
I said to the woman, then straightened her out,
"The reason I called my friend Monkey," I said,
"Is he doesn't like being called Samuel instead."
The woman responded with fire in her eyes,
And told me she saw through my racist disguise,
"You called your friend Monkey," she said, "'cause he's black,
And now I'm demanding you take those words back."
I told her I wouldn't, explaining why not,
And said it was due to the surname he'd got,
Although she'd been wrong, I applauded her spunk,
Then told her the surname of Samuel was Monk,
She blushed with embarrassment, hiding her face,
And said she was sorry with admirable grace,
She smiled, we shook hands, then she went quite berserk,
As I said: "Come on, Sambo. Let's get back to work."

Graham Eastaugh 29/3/03

# Comic capers

Batman and Robin were up for a knobbin',
But Catwoman wouldn't comply,
They wanted to poke her, and so did the Joker,
The Riddler could not reason why,
He thought she was rough, and not pretty enough,
And added: "But not only that,
My mum told me this: have a life full of bliss,
But never have sex with a cat."
Batman said: "So? What does that old bag know?
I've got to get out of these tights,
I don't care what you say, at the end of the day,
I'm shagging her one of these nights."
Robin said: "How?" Then he screamed: "Holy cow!"
When he noticed the size of his tool,
Batman just winked, whereas Catwoman blinked,
While the Joker made fun of it all,
They then stopped for luncheon, and Batman's Bat-truncheon,
Was carefully hidden from view,
Catwoman looked narked because Batman remarked:
"I'm saving this baby for *you*."
Catwoman said: "Stop. I don't care what you've got,
I'm sleeping alone in my bed."
She switched off the light, wished the others 'Good night',
And then sucked on a Penguin instead.

Graham Eastaugh 15/7/01

# Bare necessities

While watching TV on occasional nights,
I've found myself facing unusual sights,
I say they're unusual; that's not quite the case,
It's more like they're normal, but in the wrong place,
I'm talking of musical acts that I see,
In video clips when I watch MTV,
Of female performers all strutting their stuff,
Whose singing apparel seems barely enough,
Whoever the artist, they're stripped to the skin,
Apart from bikinis, the naked look's in,
It's not that these images leave me aghast,
It's just that I'm thinking of days from the past,
I'm thinking of yesteryear's pop music stars,
Parading around in their knickers and bras,
My memory clock then began to unwind,
The following images then came to mind:
I can't see the Weather Girls looking too quaint,
Or Mama Cass pretty a picture to paint,
And moving my frightening thoughts on a smidgen,
I cringe for the pianist in Lieutenant Pigeon,
If singing today, they could *not* sell their arts,
As only 'presentable' girls make the charts,
I can't see the Nolans with nude fronts and backs,
Or Cilla Black prancing about in her cacks,
And what such a sad set of values we've got,
Where content means little, but image the lot,
Where vocals aren't crucial, as long as you're 'cool',
Where marketability supersedes all,
But that's how it is; it's the way of the world,
And now as my ode is completely unfurled,
I've reached the conclusion we've got it all wrong,
That now it's a case of the look, not the song.

Graham Eastaugh 27/7/01

187

# Swings and roundabouts

Whatever became of those halcyon days,
When lives were lived out in more innocent ways,
With each public move not for everyone's eyes,
When people would live less like crazed blue-arsed flies?
When people would talk face-to-face, not online,
When courtesy levels weren't deep in decline,
When failure was not always twinned with excuse,
And people were less prone to verbal abuse?
When judges had power and schoolteachers respect,
When street violence wasn't the norm to detect,
When Channel 4 still had some dignity left,
And no one had heard of identity theft?
When pensioners didn't fear walking our streets,
When life produced far fewer benefit cheats,
When character counted for more than just looks,
And prisons would comfortably house all our crooks?
But not everything has gone downhill with time,
Our medical knowledge is now at its prime,
We've gradually softened our bigoted views,
And pavements as dumping grounds dogs no more use,
And hooliganism at football's now rare,
Most people have adequate finance to spare,
The minimum wage has been given the nod,
And Sundays are no longer shut down for 'God',
Modernity offers up both cons and pros,
And that's how life's been in the past I suppose,
Some changes bring blessings, yet others a curse,
Some act for the better, though others for worse,
A half-empty glass is a glass that's half-full,
It's all down to which way our attitudes pull,
We all have our views on what change in life brings,
But roundabouts tend to be offset by swings.

Graham Eastaugh 4/6/07

# Storm in a D-cup

Most of us like to improve how we look,
But some things are going too far in my book,
I understand make-up, and doing our hair,
And all sorts of items of clothing to wear,
I'm okay with tattoos, and likewise hair gel,
I even accept body-piercing as well,
But one thing that leaves me not one bit impressed,
Is women who practise enlarging their breasts,
I'm not talking natural ways to enhance,
But silicone substances used as implants,
Their size might increase by employing this craft,
There's only one problem: they look bloody daft,
I know that it's done for improving appeal,
But who wants to play with some breasts that aren't real?
If human attraction is all about size,
Then why is it no one enlarges their eyes?
We are what we are, and that's how it should stay,
However we're made, nature meant it that way,
Whatever our figure, the face always fits,
There's more to a woman than bloody great tits,
So, girls all around, please don't tear me apart,
I know that your knockers are close to your heart,
I'm fully aware that you've minds of your own,
But take my advice, and just leave 'em alone!

Graham Eastaugh 5/3/00

# The return of the magnificent one

Religion's a favourite topic of mine,
Discussing events that are deemed as divine,
Debating the question of: is there a God?
And if there is, isn't the lack of proof odd?
I'm not a believer in Christ or the Lord,
Though, clearly, all other views can't be ignored,
But say that I'm wrong, and my thoughts are off track,
What's going to happen when Jesus comes back?
The subject can sometimes be somewhat mind-numbing,
But how will things pan out on Christ's Second Coming?
What part of the world will he choose to go first?
And will unbelievers like me become cursed?
Will people believe him, and hear out his views?
Will Nike or adidas sponsor his shoes?
Will all that he asks for be his at a wish?
If we cook the chips, will he bring round the fish?
We'll love him at parties, as long as there's water,
And who'll be the first to allege she's his daughter?
And if he plays football, whoever his boss is,
Will surely not play him in goal, facing crosses?
And will he return as an ordinary fella?
And will his appearance destroy Uri Geller?
Will modern day folk be a little abusive?
And which of the tabloids will get an exclusive?
And if he's our Saviour, he's surely too late,
He's got such a lot of hard work on his plate,
None of us knows what's ahead I suppose,
I guess it's an instance of: God only knows.

Graham Eastaugh 17/9/99

# Wondrous stories

I once knew a man with incredible skill,
Whatever the task, he could do it at will,
But not only do it, he'd always be best,
And always be one step ahead of the rest,
The brainiest person the world's ever seen,
He'd got ten degrees by the age of thirteen,
And what a great life of romancing he's led,
He's had over twenty Miss Worlds share his bed,
He ran like the wind, and a long time ago,
He even made steam locomotives look slow,
His cricketing prowess was hard to believe,
He twice scored a ton from just ten balls received,
And every opponent at boxing he'd lick,
And one time while fishing, he caught Moby Dick,
When living in China, he wrestled a tiger,
And one day he climbed the North face of the Eiger,
He acted in movies, and mixed with the stars,
And once built a spaceship, then flew it to Mars,
He used to lend money to Jean Paul Getty,
And while in Tibet, he shook hands with the yeti,
He sat down to dinner with Presley last year,
And no one in history has drunk so much beer,
He played lead guitar for the band, the Police,
And under a pseudonym, wrote War and Peace,
These stories enthralled me, but one thing I found:
Not one single witness was ever around,
Though some of his tales might have sounded absurd,
They must have been true, 'cause he gave me his word,
I'm nobody's fool, so they can't have been lies,
And no one can pull the wool over my eyes,
But maybe I'm wrong, and this bloke was just full,
Of stuff that comes out the back end of a bull.

Graham Eastaugh 20/3/99

# Reasons to be cheerful

While thinking of life, sitting on my behind,
I reached the conclusion it's all in the mind,
It's not about talent, achievement or wealth,
Degree of intelligence, standing or health,
It's all about state of mind; feeling at ease,
Of feeling relaxed, being easy to please,
Of being untroubled, and not at all stressed,
Forgetting the worst, and enjoying the best,
We think we're so clever, but how can this be?
We're mostly unstable, or is it just me?
We call ourselves bright, but when all's done and said,
We seem to fall short on contentment of head,
And what *is* intelligence? Content of brain?
Or seeking out sunshine where others see rain?
The more that we learn, then the more for us bad,
For aiming too high only drives people mad,
It seems very few of us know how to cope,
With keeping reality separate from hope,
And why do we worry our lifetime away?
And why is it few of us live for the day?
I seem to be banging my head on a wall,
It seems to me best to have no brains at all,
One can't be unhappy, or jealous from greed,
If no brain's required, I've got just what I need?

Graham Eastaugh 25/10/99

# Looks familiar

Darwin surmised we descended from apes,
I'd never before been convinced of this view,
I'd always assumed it the utmost of japes,
I couldn't believe that his theory was true,
But recent events made me think once again,
That maybe old Charlie indeed got it right,
And maybe his sterling work wasn't in vain,
So all my suspicions began to take flight,
I went to a wildlife park; Longleat in fact,
And studied the animals strolling about,
With windows all shut, and some sandwiches packed,
I went on to see things to cause me such doubt,
The lions were ferocious, and scared me to death,
The elephants couldn't half pile up the dung,
And all of the llamas had terrible breath,
The mother hyenas all laughed at their young,
And then came the moment that altered my thoughts,
I'd never believed that my mind could be changed,
I suddenly realised that Darwin's reports,
Were not from a man so completely deranged,
I reached the enclosure that housed the baboons,
My mind totted up evolutional sums,
Their general behaviour was that of buffoons,
And all seemed obsessed with their willies and bums,
Most had erections, and all of them fleas,
I saw masturbation all over the place,
They bickered a lot, and weren't easy to please,
And one had an arse like a humanoid's face,
I owed an apology; Charles knew the score,
*He'd* always been right, and *I'd* always been wrong,
My memory told me I'd seen this before,
We're all bloody monkeys, and were all along.

Graham Eastaugh 8/10/99

# Living on the edge

I'm always bemused by the way we view fear,
The way we interpret it never seems clear,
For some of us thrive on it; others not so,
And all of us work at not letting it show,
We have things like funfairs to generate dread,
Or, should we prefer, bungee jumping instead,
Yet most of the time, we wish danger away,
And strive to keep anything frightening at bay,
And how can a woman be scared of a spider,
But not of the birth of the baby inside her?
And why do we worry when taking a test,
But don't give a thought about what we ingest?
I'm constantly baffled by nature's design,
How human security walks a fine line,
We long for excitement, but only so much,
When thrill turns to fright, it gets too hot to touch,
If only we knew all the ways of the mind,
We'd learn how to leave all our worries behind,
I think I've an answer, but then again not,
I simply conclude we're a funny old lot.

Graham Eastaugh 24/3/00

# An enduring image

I'd like to believe I'm a fairly nice chap,
I live and let live, and wish no one mishap,
But sitting alone just the night before last,
A very large doubt on this viewpoint was cast,
I thought of my days from the start until now,
Recalling all memories my mind would allow,
But each different era my brain would evoke,
I couldn't shake off one particular bloke,
Whatever the time, he would *always* be there,
I just couldn't get the guy out of my hair,
I've always watched telly whenever I can,
But all of my life I've been dogged by this man,
He first got my goat with objectionable noise,
By singing a song about two little boys,
And one thing he'd do that got right up my snout,
Was holding this board that he'd wobble about,
Whatever the year, there'd be *me* watching *him,*
Painting a picture; or teaching to swim,
But why so much airtime? I haven't a clue,
Unless it's the size of his didgeridoo?
He made silly noises that took some believing,
He'd sometimes break out into weird heavy breathing,
And just when I thought that's as bad as it gets,
He shows up again interfering with pets,
You've probably twigged - I'm a big fan of his,
As *he* might have said: can you tell who it is?
I can't help believing I'd feel less forlorn,
If only Rolf Harris had never been born.

Graham Eastaugh 7/3/01

# Bad language

The teachers at school used to treat me so rough,
They said that my English just weren't good enough,
They said when I left school, I'd soon come a cropper,
'Cause things what I wrote shew I weren't bought up proper,
But I worked really hard, and done ever so well,
I brought a new dictionary, learnt how to spell,
They told me my usage of tenses was poor,
The truth is I couldn't of tried any more,
They said I was finished before I begun,
Of future job prospects, I didn't have none,
About punctuation, they said mines' a crime,
I can't work that out, 'cause I'm always on time,
I wasn't put off; I was much too resilient,
I know it sounds brash, but I done really brilliant,
I made them look foolish; too clever by half,
With egg on there faces, I got the last laugh,
'Cause now I'm much older, the future's much brighter,
My diction is great, and I'm such a good writer,
They said with my English, I'd not get along,
But as you can see from this ode, they was wrong.

Graham Eastaugh 13/3/99

# Altered images

I'm glad, in one way, I was born when I was,
I'm pleased I was born in the Sixties because,
Whatever we did, we were left well alone,
With memories of yesteryear solely our own,
We took the odd black-and-white photograph then,
When special events took place now and again,
But, other than that, we had nothing at all,
In terms of pictorial thoughts to recall,
The advent of video changed life so much,
With memories in motion it put us in touch,
So now we record any moment we choose,
And that's why I hold my aforementioned views,
I'm glad to forget certain days from my past,
Embarrassing moments to leave me aghast,
'Cause that's what they are when we see them for real,
They never seem anything like we'd once feel,
Without any evidence proving us wrong,
Our fictional memories are potently strong,
Whatever the truth is, our memories err,
And see better times than they actually were,
And think about some of the things of tomorrow,
The kids of the day, and their moments of sorrow,
The intimate viewing to set tongues a-wagging,
Like video clips of their grandparents shagging,
Their mums being tarts, and their dads being twats,
And anyone under sixteen being brats,
Including themselves, though they'd rather forget,
Or watching an aunt stripping off for a bet,
My point is the longer we are in the tooth,
The better we are at reshaping the truth,
For accurate replays the video's king,
But recall of choice is a much better thing.

Graham Eastaugh 5/11/01

# Puss in Boots

The owl and the pussycat went to see,
If the owl was expecting a baby,
The chemist said: "Wee in this jar for me,"
Then after a test he said: "Maybe."
He said to the pussycat: "Don't think I'm rude,
But isn't it strange that your partner's a bird?
And don't think of me as an old-fashioned prude,
But surely a nice pussy should be preferred?"
The pussycat said that he's unlike the rest,
And added he once had a fling with a goat,
He said that the two of them one day undressed,
And made love in a beautiful pea-green boat,
The chemist said: "Sorry, it just isn't right,
A cat should be only in love with a cat,
It's not that I want to sound so impolite,
But crossbreeding's wrong, it's as simple as that."
The pussycat said: "But a cow I once knew,
Was happily married for years to a mouse,
Their living together caused little ado,
And though they've now split, they still share the same house,
The mouse is now courting a pig as it goes."
The chemist said: "Stop!" and sarcastically laughed,
"And they danced by the light of the moon I suppose?"
And the pussycat said: "Now you're just being daft."

Graham Eastaugh 23/11/01

# Gobbledegook

"I can't seem to find you a window," he said,
"I've so much to do more important instead,
I've set up a think-tank tomorrow, you see,
A brainstorming session with others and me,
The company big guns are coming to town,
Between you and me, something big's going down,
A marketing sea change is most what we need,
This product's *my* baby; it has to succeed,
I thought we'd adopt an aggressive position,
And get into bed with our main opposition,
We're milking a cash cow, of that there's no doubt,
We just need to maximise getting milk out,
We need to be streamlining; leading the field,
We need contract wins from the big cheeses sealed,
We want our competitors left in our wake,
We need to expand on our slice of the cake."
He looked slightly flustered, and puffed out his cheeks,
And told me he'd had trouble sleeping for weeks,
My views on the matter he finally sought,
"What absolute bollocks he's talking," I thought.

Graham Eastaugh 25/5/01

# The man in the mirror

The face in the mirror looked haggard and old,
A lifetime of hardship was there to behold,
His eyes told a story of terminal chore,
The face of a man who could suffer no more,
Impossible odds where there used to be hope,
The look of a man now unable to cope,
A fear of the future that once held no dread,
The days when he used to know laughter instead,
His image reflected a look of despair,
Of someone who fought but could no longer care,
Where once there was sheen his expression was blank,
He didn't have any more gas in the tank,
He looked like a man with invisible tears,
A person who pined for his halcyon years,
He'd given his all but he couldn't keep pace,
And utter exhaustion was etched on his face,
It tortured me looking at someone so sad,
The fact I was helpless to aid him so mad,
And one thing specifically troubled me so,
He seemed to remind me of someone I know,
I know what you're thinking - you've spotted the link,
But maybe you're not quite as smart as you think,
An old man was standing behind me, you see,
I bet you a tenner you thought it was me.

Graham Eastaugh 20/1/02

# The kids are alright?

Everyone's bound by the laws of the land,
We shouldn't do things that our rulers have banned,
And every so often, the changes they ring,
I wonder what new laws the future might bring?
Historically speaking, it's not long ago,
A whole set of different laws were on show,
Women and men didn't share the same boat,
For women weren't even permitted to vote,
It wasn't so easy to file for divorce,
A marriage was forced into lasting the course,
Abnormal relationships had to be hidden,
As all homosexual acts were forbidden,
Whatever the laws are, our morals reflect,
If something's deemed legal, that's what we expect,
What once was appalling, today is okay,
I then looked ahead to a different day:
I'm certain the age of consent will come down,
So criminal acts become 'fooling around',
And who's to say one day, by popular rule,
A paedophile won't be a monster at all?
I certainly hope that this doesn't come true,
But what if our tolerance levels accrue?
Will child abuse no longer be judged a crime?
And paedophiles now just ahead of their time?

Graham Eastaugh 30/1/00

# The proof of the pudding...

The Loch Ness monster, and 'saucers' from space,
And Big Foot parading all over the place,
The yeti patrolling the slopes of Tibet,
So how is it nobody's seen any yet?
Of course, over time, we've had 'sightings' galore,
But each seems to have a significant flaw,
I'd love to believe that these things all exist,
But being a sceptic's too hard to resist,
Pictorial 'evidence' never seems clear,
All footage was shot from not anywhere near,
But not only that; all these video takes,
Were filmed by observers with terrible shakes,
And over the years, we've seen many a con,
Like someone on film with a monkey suit on,
And photos of 'Nessie' afloat in the bath,
And 'spaceships' espied on a distant flight path,
And who can be sure of the Roswell affair?
Of film that was shot with immaculate care?
In fact, so much care that, instead of hard proof,
It only adds fuel to supporting the truth,
The truth is the proof is there's nothing at all,
They're fanciful myths, but we're easy to fool,
If these things exist, don't you find it strange how,
With all that's to gain, we've not proved it by now?

Graham Eastaugh 12/10/99

# Whose life is it, anyway?

Euthanasia - is it a sin?
Well, certainly so in the eyes of the law,
Of course, it's an argument no one can win,
For neither result is what one would hope for,
Some say it's immoral, and others good sense,
As long as it's voluntary, why should we care?
The full implications are simply immense,
But isn't our judgement on others unfair?
If someone decides that their life's not worth living,
Should nature prevail, and demise have to wait?
And why should it be that we're so unforgiving,
In letting a person decide their own fate?
Nobody wants to see death without reason,
I'm not advocating demise at a whim,
But why is it deemed as a high moral treason,
In cases where futures are desperately grim?
We view it humane to put animals down,
As misery ended; a peaceful conclusion,
So why should a human life cause such a frown?
And why such a right for this legal intrusion?
If someone's in pain of the very worst kind,
Where's the incentive for carrying on?
Round-the-clock agony? Losing your mind?
And heartbroken relatives so put upon?
It's always so easy to judge other folk,
But all views against euthanasia put,
Would surely so rapidly go up in smoke,
If one day the boot should decide to change foot?

Graham Eastaugh 28/9/99

# Ask a silly question...

"A penny for your thoughts," said the beautiful girl,
I told her she'd certainly *not* want to know,
"Try me," she said, so I gave it a whirl,
I opened my heart, and enlightened her so:
"This woman I know - I was thinking of *her*,
The two of us naked, and lying in bed,
Embroiled in a night of hot passion we were,
And, Jesus, could she give magnificent head!
She went like a train; she was dirty all right,
Whatever I did, she kept screaming for more,
We went hammer and tongs at it right through the night,
I made the bitch cry she was feeling so sore."
The beautiful girl asked me: "What was her name?"
I paused as I didn't quite know what to do,
I told her that she and this girl looked the same,
"To be more precise," I then told her, "it's you."
She stepped back in horror; I came to mishap,
She rather aggressively took me to task,
She called an arsehole, and gave me a slap,
"If you don't want to know," I said, "why bloody ask?"
She stormed off and screamed she had no more to say,
I found out she had a bad temper, and how!
The following sentence I shouted her way:
"You owe me a penny, you frigid old cow!"

Graham Eastaugh 3/6/01

# Much ado about nothing?

I don't know a thing about some things in life,
Like how many blades has a Swiss army knife?
But one thing I'm sure of: I'm not out of touch,
In thinking that some of us worry too much,
Life can be short, so there's no time to waste,
We shouldn't have fears that are maybe misplaced,
Things we consume is to what I allude,
The subject: genetically modified food,
Panic abounds over problems we've got,
It may be with reason, but probably not,
The message on GM foods: people beware,
I can't help believing it's purely hot air,
It's not that all warnings I choose to ignore,
It's just that I seem to have heard it before,
With BSE, CJD, beef on the bone,
Why can't they leave us meat-eaters alone?
They've scared us of eggs, and of milk, and of wine,
A cow is taboo, but a chicken leg's fine,
Whatever we eat, we can never be sure,
But think of the things that our stomachs endure,
I mix with a crowd who are ever so nice,
They're mostly dung beetles, to be more precise,
They live a hard life, but they don't care one bit,
They're all in good health, yet their meals are all shit,
So why should we all start to feel highly strung,
When clearly it's quite safe to eat our own dung?
GM foods might put the wind up some nerds,
But surely it's better than scoffing your turds?

Graham Eastaugh 19/5/99

# Degrees of exploitation

I came home one night from a trip into town,
I felt quite relieved; it was bucketing down,
I took off my coat, then the weight off my feet,
Then Plonker the parrot I'd cheerfully greet:
"Who's a pretty boy, then?" I said to the bird,
But Plonker's reply was a shock, every word,
He didn't say 'Plonker' or 'Pieces of eight,'
He just said the following, looking irate:
"Don't patronise me with that pretty boy stuff,
You think I'm all smiles, but I've had quite enough,
This cage is like prison; I never get out,
I've got bugger all to be happy about,
I've no one like Wilberforce fighting my cause,
Or Abraham Lincoln rewriting the laws,
And unlike the Negroes, my plight's been forgotten,
I'm no better off than those Blacks picking cotton,
And Hammy the hamster - he's in the same boat,
You've got him at work on a treadmill I note,
Your kitten's the same - what a way to exist,
He begs for his food like he's Oliver Twist!"
My pet parrot's outburst was such a surprise,
And, being quite honest, had opened my eyes,
His knowledge of history took me aback,
I felt somewhat dumbstruck, and much on the rack,
I tried to be civil, suppressing my rage,
Unfurling a blanket to cover his cage,
He lives in my house like the hamster and cat,
So no bloody parrot can treat me like *that,*
I switched off the light, and went upstairs to bed,
And thought of the things that my parrot had said,
I couldn't accept his opinion of me,
So later that week I had parrot for tea.

Graham Eastaugh 5/8/01

# Something about you baby I like

You look like a princess; your figure's divine,
It makes me deliriously happy you're mine,
Your heart's made of gold sent from heaven above,
Your voice like the beautiful song of a dove,
You cook the most fantastic meals ever made,
Your sexual technique puts the rest in the shade,
You don't mind me coming home pissed every night,
And think all my bits on the side are all right,
You don't mind me playing golf six days a week,
You quite like me giving your nipples a tweak,
You don't mind me spending more time with my chums,
At times of the month when your period comes,
You happily sew on my buttons for me,
Whatever I'm saying, you always agree,
You do all the shopping, and keep the house warm,
And take out your teeth for some acts you perform,
You don't mind the telly is only for sport,
Apart from those filthy cassettes I've just bought,
You don't mind me being in comatose states,
Or selling you sometimes to some of my mates,
Whatever I think of as perfect you've got,
There's something about you I like such a lot,
Your utter devotion to me you have sworn,
There's only one problem - you haven't been born.

Graham Eastaugh 2/8/01

# Villains of the peace

The leaves of the trees gently danced on the breeze,
The sun, slowly rising, was eager to please,
The temperature such that the day was ideal,
The beauty of nature was almost surreal,
There wasn't a hint of a cloud in the sky,
A cat looked bemused as a fieldmouse skipped by,
The birds in the bushes were singing away,
A family of rabbits all rolled in the hay,
"Cock-a-doodle-doo," crowed the cock before dawn,
"Baa," said the sheep as his offspring was born,
The cow in the field then proceeded to moo,
The dove flying overhead started to coo,
"Oink," said the pig as he snouted around,
The ducks by the pond made a loud quacking sound,
The sheepdog was barking while chasing his tail,
The horses all neighed on an ear-piercing scale,
The farmer awoke and was clutching his head,
Regretting he wasn't teetotal instead,
He shouted out loudly while hurling a cup,
"Why don't you noisy cunts shut the fuck up!"

Graham Eastaugh 3/10/01

# Seeing is believing

They say you don't know what you've got till it's gone,
I found out the hard way it's perfectly true,
The instant it vanished, I stumbled upon,
A chance to reflect a more accurate view,
Life must have been great many years in the past,
So how come I didn't interpret it so?
I had what I had, and that's how things would last,
My being was blessed, but I just didn't know,
Whatever our treasures, we always want more,
We rarely appreciate things that we've got,
Our natural blessings we somehow ignore,
We struggle to see what's important, and not,
We all know in theory the value of health,
But take it for granted, as if it's our right,
We focus so much on material wealth,
Of things most important we seem to lose sight,
If healthy and happy, you've all that you need,
It baffles me how we don't notice the fact,
It's only in hindsight the saying's agreed,
And only when health is no longer intact,
If I could give proof, then believe me I would,
To find out the answer, you'll just have to wait,
Whatever you're told, it will do you no good,
You won't understand till a moment too late.

Graham Eastaugh 6/3/00

# Easy life

The kids of today, they don't know they've been born,
Everything comes to them laid on a plate,
Their cushy lives fill me with anger and scorn,
It's not that I'm jealous; just bloody irate,
Others might say I should not feel aggrieved,
Just 'cause I've had it so terribly tough,
But life's just a breeze from the day they're conceived,
The fact is they're not made to graft hard enough,
Right from the moment I came from the womb,
I'd not got a pot I could piss in,
Another misfortune that filled me with gloom:
I noticed my teeth were all missing,
I worked down the mines twenty-five hours a day,
My hands would be covered in blisters,
And all for a farthing a week as my pay,
To share with my twenty-three brothers and sisters,
Father would beat me; he'd torture and maim,
My mum was a slave to the cooker,
And when she was too pissed to go on the game,
I'd dress up in drag and then work as a hooker,
Riddled with Aids, I would sleep on the street,
Breakfast and lunch were just pipe dreams for me,
'Cause eight days a week I'd have nothing to eat,
Apart from a boot in my face for my tea,
I fought in both wars, but what thanks have I got,
From the youngsters who've reaped the reward?
There's one other thing that I nearly forgot,
I bullshit like fuck when I'm utterly bored.

Graham Eastaugh 28/11/98

# Painful reminder

The teenager said to her granddad one day,
That *her* age group did things a different way,
How *her* generation pushed fashion ahead,
And put all the trends of the old days to bed,
She pulled up her T-shirt to bear out her case,
Revealing a couple of tattoos in place,
She said to her granddad they opened the door,
To trend-setting ways never witnessed before,
Her navel was pierced as, indeed, was her tongue,
She said this was strictly in vogue for the young,
She said that these things were refreshingly new,
However, her granddad then challenged this view,
He told her she wasn't as smart as she thought,
A valuable lesson she had to be taught,
He told her to not judge her elders so fast,
Instructing her sternly of days from the past,
He spoke of his youth, and the friends he once had,
The tone of his voice now emotionally sad,
He talked of how piercing was commonplace then,
Though shrapnel it was for the bravest of men,
He said that *her* lot didn't know they'd been born,
His lecture continued with heightening scorn:
"And don't talk to me about flaming tattoos,
I've seen 'em before in the war with the Jews."
His granddaughter sat with a tear in her eye,
She felt quite ashamed, though she didn't know why,
She'd done nothing wrong, so she wasn't to blame,
Her granddad had put her to terrible shame,
He reached out his arm, and he gave her a hug,
She gave him a smile, and her shoulders a shrug,
He told her it's not that she owed him a debt,
He just thought it something she shouldn't forget.

Graham Eastaugh 11/10/01

# Reality bites

Think of the animal parts that we eat,
Aside from the regular cuts of prime meat,
The various sections on which we may dine,
And see if your views are in common with mine,
These days, of course, we know what to expect,
The taste of all things has already been checked,
But someone in history had to go first,
And see if a part be for better or worse,
Who the fuck first thought of eating sheep's eyes?
And how did the idea of gonads arise?
And why would an ox be deprived of its tail?
And which desperado first sampled a snail?
Shellfish and lobsters, and fish from the sea,
Brains of a monkey and stuff from a bee,
Livers and kidneys, and birds from the sky,
Is anything out there we've still left to try?
No creature is safe on this planet called Earth,
Whatever's around, we'll find out what it's worth,
At least we don't eat the insides of a horse,
That's doner kebab meat excepted, of course.

Graham Eastaugh 21/11/01

# Who's that bastard in the black?

No one gets stick like a football referee,
Their every mistake is for all eyes to see,
When anger's in order it's always the same,
Whatever goes wrong, the ref's always to blame,
They know that's the way - they're the scorn of the mob,
And being unpopular's part of the job,
So given the fact these conditions are clear,
What makes a referee choose that career?
The answer's quite simple in my estimation,
The chance for dictatorship's my explanation,
It's all about power and being in charge,
And that's why there's so many knobheads at large,
It isn't the game that appeals to them most,
But rather the power that comes with the post,
From kick-off to end they have total control,
They briefly adopt a significant role,
And here's where my theory begins to take shape,
A referee's job is their only escape,
From normal existence, in which they expect,
Complete anonymity - zero respect,
There'll be some exceptions, but mostly it's true,
The buzz of the job's telling folk what to do,
For other than times when a match is in play,
Who gives a toss what a ref's got to say?
The job's tailor-made for an absolute nerd,
And someone who used to be bullied's preferred,
They're wannabe cops, traffic wardens likewise,
They love cutting prominent folk down to size,
Positions of power attract certain sorts,
An urge for control's uppermost in their thoughts,
They can't be ignored if they're pulling the strings,
And that's why there's so many berks running things.

Graham Eastaugh 18/11/01

213

# Cheap trick

The young woman threw back the covers at dawn,
Her boyfriend beside her awoke with a yawn,
A look of excitement appeared on her face,
All signs of despondency lost without trace,
Today marked the end of her twenty-fourth year,
The words of her boyfriend seemed warmly sincere,
He told her he loved her in every way,
And wished many happy returns of the day,
They kissed and they cuddled; he fondled her chest,
She told him to stop as she had to get dressed,
She put on some trousers, a bra and a top,
And went about seeing what presents she'd got,
Her mum bought her slippers; her brother a scarf,
Her twin sister gave her some salts for the bath,
Her dad sent a cheque, which she couldn't believe,
She only had one present left to receive,
She turned to her boyfriend, and gave him a smile,
And told him she'd open *his* gift in a while,
But all of a sudden, her mood took a fall,
He told her *his* present was nothing at all,
"You'd better be taking the piss," she replied,
Apparently calm, although seething inside,
He told her he wasn't, but why should she care?
And offered the following viewpoints to share:
"I *thought* you were quite insecure in the head,
I *thought* you were boring, and clueless in bed,
I *thought* you were scheming to get in the club,
And *thought* you were shagging that bloke down the pub,
I *thought* you were always as pissed as a fart,
I *thought* you were starting to act like a tart,
I *thought* you were so bloody fat you could bounce,
And *thought* that you told me the *thought* is what counts."

Graham Eastaugh 28/10/01

# Prying eyes

The universe stretches beyond our perception,
Our planet just one of a massive collection,
We think we're alone, but we don't really know,
The following images worry me so:
What if an alien race is out there,
Watching us somehow with consummate care,
The human race being their preoccupation,
Keeping us all under close observation?
And if that's the case, I'm not sure I can cope,
Like fleas are to us under huge microscope,
I value my privacy; dignity too,
I don't want a crowd for whatever I do,
I don't want some alien poking his snout,
In times of my life when my goolies are out,
I'm not being awkward; it's just how it goes,
I need my own space when I'm picking my nose,
I don't want an audience taking a peep,
At things I get up to with underage sheep,
I don't want it known that my underwear's frilly,
Or anyone having a laugh at my willy,
I don't want my private life screened on TV,
On extraterrestrial planets, you see,
I don't want my every move being assessed,
I don't want exposure when not at my best,
So if there are aliens out there in space,
With hi-tech surveillance equipment in place,
Who've witnessed a few of the things I've just said,
Don't tell anyone until after I'm dead.

Graham Eastaugh 17/5/01

# Too little, too late

Most of us don't seem to like giving praise,
We're so often driven by negative ways,
We seem so reluctant to speak as we feel,
True feelings we hold in our hearts we conceal,
There seems to be some sort of unwritten rule,
That compliments given are somewhat uncool,
We might view a person the nicest around,
But seem to take pleasure in putting them down,
With people we don't really like it's the same,
We speak fairly *well* to a less-admired name,
Yet no one can ever take time to relax,
For opposite comments are made behind backs,
We all have desire to be spoken of well,
We think that we know where we stand, but can't tell,
The words that are spoken so often deceive,
For how many hearts are worn open on sleeve?
There's only one sure way of learning the truth,
One single scenario giving us proof,
Of what people think of us, honest and true,
Of how other people might hold us in view,
I might be mistaken, but see what you think,
But kind words are rare while we're still in the pink,
It seems such a shame, and I can't explain why,
But praise rarely comes till the moment we die.

Graham Eastaugh 25/3/00

# Every second counts

So here I am stuck in the last chance saloon,
I guess they'll be calling for last orders soon,
The bar's really packed with no bar staff on show,
I'm dying for one final drink till I go,
The hands on the clock seem unusually fast,
The last chance saloon's landlord shows up at last,
I've worked myself up into panicking mode,
I just want a chance to have one for the road,
Still nothing has happened while yet more time passes,
The landlord announces they've run out of glasses,
I'm screaming inside though I try to stay cool,
I desperately want one more refill, that's all,
To be this impatient's not naturally me,
It's just that my thirst is so urgent, you see,
There's always tomorrow to do the same thing,
But who can be sure what tomorrow might bring?
The landlord is totally blameless it's true,
That no one else drinks at the speed that I do,
I've missed the last bell but I shouldn't complain,
As long as I witness last orders again.

Graham Eastaugh 17/4/02

# Modern romance

The elderly couple, so obviously proud,
Occasioned to question their grandson aloud,
The youngster was all ears and eager to please,
Just one year away from his GCSEs,
His grandmother said: "Are you yet walking out,
With someone you feel extra special about,
An affable damsel who's captured your heart,
A time in your life at which courting might start?"
His grandfather added, to make things more clear:
"Is anyone presently nibbling your ear?
Or maybe you're necking whilst dating perchance?
Or taking the floor for a smooch as you dance?"
His grandson immediately gave his reply,
A look of befuddlement showed in his eye,
His answer was what inactivity brings,
He said he'd been doing not one of those things,
His grandmother countered: "Then what do you do,
With all your spare time in a day to get through?"
He thought it quite strange that she wanted to know,
But did what she asked and thus answered her so:
"I'm getting things on with a hot bitch at school,
Who's seriously wicked, so everything's cool,
I'm out every night and don't come home till late,
And lately I've also been banging her mate."
His grandparents smiled as the boy turned away,
His grandmother then had a few words to say,
She said to her spouse as this ditty unfurls:
"I think he was saying he doesn't like girls."

Graham Eastaugh 5/7/02

# Masters of invention

Just think of the progress we humans have made,
From humble beginnings, we've now made the grade,
Technology; science; we've mastered the lot,
And all through the brilliant minds that we've got,
But just as I started to feel rather smug,
A string to my conscience occasioned to tug,
The following thought was presented to me:
Without *my* intelligence, where would we be?
I suddenly felt like the biggest of berks,
Concluding I don't know how anything works,
I've all the mod cons, but should something break down,
I'm useless, apart from producing a frown,
I'd like to believe I'm of reasonable mind,
That most of the planet's of similar kind,
So maybe you'd not disagree with my view,
We owe such a lot to a relative few,
If all throughout time had *my* content of brain,
We'd shelter in caves to keep out of the rain,
We'd travel by foot, and no ailments we'd heal,
We wouldn't have even invented the wheel,
The next time you find yourself praising our race,
For all the developments put into place,
How human achievement's come such a long way,
Just answer this question: what part did *you* play?

Graham Eastaugh 1/2/00

# Rags to riches

Why is it fashion shows draw such attention,
When clearly they're nothing but acts of pretension?
They're so superficial; significance small,
And egos aside, they're of no use at all,
Yet up on the catwalk where pretty things strut,
Parading themselves in the latest of cut,
Attraction seems vast of celebrity kind,
And life in the real world gets left well behind,
The latest designs attract widespread acclaim,
And bring their creators considerable fame,
The interest attached to these shows is immense,
But surely they're nothing but pointless events?
For how many times are these clothes ever seen?
Apart from occasions when stars of the screen,
Appear in their splendour in front of the press,
With nothing to boast but impractical dress?
To me these extravagant shows are a crime,
The truth is they're simply a huge waste of time,
So why they continue I haven't a clue,
I guess it's a question of: who's fooling who?

Graham Eastaugh 11/2/00

# Hopping mad

Tommy the toad was extremely unhappy,
His mood was becoming increasingly snappy,
His rising blood pressure was bad for his health,
He seemed to be always explaining himself,
He lived by a pond with a commune of frogs,
But keeping his cool was the hardest of slogs,
He felt so frustrated, and desperately sad,
The frogs by the pond had been driving him mad,
They didn't believe he was really a toad,
They acted the same, and no difference showed,
They called him a frog, and they wouldn't concede,
That Tommy the toad wasn't one of their breed,
Tommy went wild, but the frogs wouldn't stop,
They said he was green, and he had a frog's hop,
He croaked like a frog, and his eyeballs bulged out,
He had to be one of their kind, without doubt,
Tommy accepted they looked quite the same,
They acted alike, but were different in name,
The frogs were accused of inciting a brawl,
He wished to be known as a toad, that was all,
The frogs wouldn't listen, and stuck to their views,
To trust in his story they'd bluntly refuse,
But this time the frogs had pushed Tommy too far,
His head blew a fuse, then he hopped to his car,
He came back and told all the frogs they would pay,
And pulled out a gun, and then blew them away,
He felt no remorse, though he knew it had been,
The worst case of toad rage the world's ever seen.

Graham Eastaugh 21/10/99

# Something else

For most of our lifetimes, we're so hard to please,
Whatever we have, it's not quite as we'd like,
We seem so unhappy to different degrees,
That most of the things that we have we dislike,
Whatever our size, and whatever our shape,
We want to be something we're presently not,
We're constantly searching for means of escape,
We yearn to have things that we now haven't got,
The same goes for families, houses and jobs,
As everyone thinks they deserve higher pay,
Most women want other tits; blokes bigger knobs,
We'd all rather things were a different way,
We want better husbands; alternative wives,
There has to be something more pleasing than this?
It's hard to believe how a human survives,
With so much contentment of mind gone amiss,
But, strangely, the moment we turn things around,
And get what we want to now render us glad,
We most likely make a familiar sound,
And want back the thing that we previously had,
It puzzles me how an intelligent breed,
Can spend so much time feeling gloomy inside,
For, most of the time, we've got all that we need,
So how come we're so often dissatisfied?

Graham Eastaugh 26/3/00

# The way things are going

The world's ever changing; the goalposts keep moving,
With everything done in the name of improving,
The way of the world with the progress we make,
And all of it done for modernity's sake,
The question I'm asking is: where will it end?
I can't see our planet reversing the trend,
I left all my thoughts of this decade behind,
The following prophecies flashed through my mind:
So many cars on the road we can't move,
Religious fanatics with more points to prove,
Kids having sex when they're seven or eight,
Community service for arson and rape,
Hard-core pornography shown on TV,
And everything watched for a pay-per-view fee,
Security guards every place that we go,
And CCTV cameras always on show,
An absolute need for insuring our health,
A widening gap between poorness and wealth,
The whole of the country obsessed with Big Brother,
And everyone everywhere suing each other,
Policemen unable to lay down the law,
And judges who don't know what prisons are for,
Teachers in schools having zero control,
More kids leaving uni to sign on the dole,
The way we live now doesn't seem strange at all,
But long in the past it would truly appal,
So bearing in mind how the changes we ring,
It's anyone's guess what the future might bring,
I'd love a sneak preview at what lies ahead,
The way of society after we're dead,
The way of the world *can't* keep changing so fast,
But part of me thinks that tomorrow won't last.

Graham Eastaugh 7/12/01

# Cock-and-bull story

Archibald Penis sat down with his wife,
And made a suggestion to alter his life,
He said to his spouse: "Shall we try for a kid?"
She nodded her head and so that's what they did,
They stripped to the skin as they rolled on the floor,
He tickled her fancy and gave her what for,
Then later that year after nine months had passed,
The Penises had a small baby at last,
They sat down again to decide on a name,
They each had a preference which turned out the same,
They both studied Kipling as much as they could,
Agreeing his cakes were exceedingly good,
And that's why they chose as a name for their son,
A name that would make him a figure of fun,
His life would be hell, though *he* couldn't be blamed,
For Rudyard Penis their son had been named,
Wherever he went he was laughed out of town,
Young Rudyard Penis could *not* live it down,
And even when drinking or smoking a spliff,
Poor Rudyard Penis was seen as a stiff,
So Rudyard Penis was lonely and sad,
A life without social acceptance he had,
Beset by frustration, his life in a trough,
He stood on a cliff top and chucked himself off.

Graham Eastaugh 7/2/03

# Criminal proceedings

"I know I did wrong," said the very young child,
Recounting the moment his faith was defiled,
He poured out his heart as his eyes filled with tears,
Confessing the loss of his innocent years,
"He told me to trust him," the boy carried on,
"So naturally all my misgivings were gone,
He said I should take on a submissive role,
Insisting I promise to not tell a soul,
I tried to be brave, but I felt so much pain,
From screaming out loudly I couldn't refrain,
He told me to be quiet and not cause a scene,
And angrily said what a bad boy I'd been,
It finally finished and then I went home,
I couldn't tell Mum and I felt so alone,
The man is respected so much around town,
My bottom was so sore I couldn't sit down,
I'm sorry I sinned, but I won't say a word,
Despite all the terrible pain I incurred,
So, Father, I beg you, forgive me my crime,"
"Don't worry, my child, I'll be gentler next time."

Graham Eastaugh 1/5/02

225

# Misguided belief

"Has it ever crossed your mind you're a wanker?" I said,
To the man with a sharp-pointed hood on his head,
With eye-holes cut out to allow him to see,
A world that appeared so repulsive to me,
I told him his views were of evil design,
His bigoted notions were way out of line,
Opinions like his belonged years in the past,
My colours then further I nailed to the mast,
I told him it wasn't a question of race,
Religion or colour of anyone's face,
It wasn't a question of title or name,
Whoever you are, we're exactly the same,
I told him the views he promoted were vile,
The filth he espoused was most hideous bile,
He stared at me fixedly; hate in his eyes,
His cowardice clear by his feeble disguise,
He reached out his arms as he called me a fool,
His hands round my throat, I was pinned to the wall,
Then just as I seriously feared for my fate,
He whispered the words: "I'm a bank robber, mate!"

Graham Eastaugh 31/12/01

# Inflated egos

The animals went in two by two,
Christ! What a gangbang that was,
There was Bodger and Stinky and Tosser and Pooh,
And a bloke from the boozer, called Oz,
I'll never forget when I first heard the news,
The story just blew me away,
My mind conjured up the most frightening of views,
Of five ugly geezers at play,
I have to point out that the girl was quite willing,
Her actions weren't taken at haste,
And though, at the time, their emotions were spilling,
It all went ahead in the very best taste,
They met at Pooh's flat; got undressed; then the order,
Was picked on the roll of some dice,
Oz wore a grin that could hardly be broader,
And Stinky, he chose to go twice,
It started quite slowly, but finished so soon,
And Bodger was awfully quick,
The air was so hot in the middle of June,
That Tosser was feeling quite sick,
They had lots of fun, but the party then finished,
Events reached a critical juncture,
The girl was no use, as their joy had diminished,
'Cause Oz stubbed his fag out, and gave her a puncture.

Graham Eastaugh 30/9/99

# For argument's sake

Now I might not be right, and if that's the case,
My heartfelt apologies forthwith I place,
But some things in life to me don't seem quite right,
The following viewpoints I now bring to light:
On certain occasions that take place on Earth,
There's always a protest to question its worth,
But something inside me spots something amiss,
The cynical side of me comes up with this:
There's many a protestor based on our shores,
But how many *really* believe in their cause?
I can't help concluding there's only a few,
The rest having nothing much better to do,
Opposers to hunting appear in their flocks,
But how many *care* for the plight of a fox?
And who gives a toss for the fate of a tree,
Or things such as GM crops; whaling at sea?
It's not my intention of causing disquiet,
But how many 'protestors' *love* a good riot?
With each innovation, a protest's in store,
But how many know what the poxy thing's for?
And even the genuine ones who *believe,*
Just what do they *really* expect to achieve?
Keeping the whole of the planet in check,
Or just wasting time being pains in the neck?

Graham Eastaugh 29/3/00

# Sliding scales

A week before Armstrong, I walked on the moon,
And once witnessed snowfall in Egypt in June,
I once saw an angel come down from the sky,
And one afternoon saw an elephant fly,
I own a pet unicorn; Horny's his name,
A wild brontosaurus I managed to tame,
I've interviewed Jesus, but stranger than that,
I've not met a woman who thinks she's not fat,
Wherever I travel, there's always the sound,
Of female intentions to lose the odd pound,
And even the skinniest women I know,
Are certain a couple of ounces should go,
But why should this happen? It seems such a shame,
I guess modern fashion is largely to blame,
Remember, it's not many years in the past,
A woman was blessed if she had a fat arse,
This whole anorexic thing drives me to sorrow,
We breed skin and bone like there'll be no tomorrow,
I'm fed up of hearing ridiculous talk,
Does nobody realise a bloke likes his pork?
So ladies all over, please heed my advice,
Eat all of the things that you fancy look nice,
And don't plan ahead to a slimming-down date,
But scoff what you like 'cause it's not worth the weight.

Graham Eastaugh 25/2/00

# The meaning of life

Why are we here? I keep asking myself,
We live and we die, and accumulate wealth,
We build and destroy, and we learn and forget,
We generate life, and then pass on the debt,
We love and we hate, and we laugh and we cry,
We fight to survive, although no one knows why,
Our blueprint's a riddle; not clearly defined,
For no one's unravelled the state of the mind,
We don't know the reason we're living on Earth,
We think we're important, but don't know our worth,
We're scared of the future, but still we persist,
We're frightened of things that don't even exist,
We're ruled by emotion; we don't have a say,
Our head knows the truth, but our heart's in the way,
Why is our balance of mind so defective?
And why can't we keep things in proper perspective?
The answer evades me, like all those before,
I try to switch off, but it's hard to ignore,
With thousands of millions of billions of stars,
We can't be alone on this planet of ours?
The best I come up with is: life can't be bad,
The reason we're here should be happy, not sad,
We're here, end of story, we're striving to climb,
We shouldn't be fearful, and live for the time,
In my way of thinking, it's live and let live,
Be true to yourself, and be quick to forgive,
Enjoying existence; avoiding all strife,
And that, I suggest, is the meaning of life.

Graham Eastaugh 26/6/99